PRAISE FOR *LIVE LIKE SEAN*

"*Live Like Sean* is a wonderful book that, like Sean himself, will stay in your heart long after you turn the final page."

—**Harlan Coben,** *New York Times* best-selling author of *The Boy from the Woods*

"A book for anyone who has ever been fiercely inspired by a child—which should be everyone."

—**Mitch Albom,** *New York Times* best-selling author of *Finding Chika*

"Through the 2014 Special Olympics USA Games, I had the great fortune to get to know Sean and his amazing family. With both a Montville and Hoboken connection, we immediately forged a friendship. I am honored and proud to have known him. Sean taught me about strength, resilience, and, mostly, patience. *Live Like Sean* provides a brief look into a life that touched so many and is a must-read about how life lessons can come from the most unexpected sources. Sean was a shining presence who impacted all who knew him, and he will be missed."

—**Buddy Valastro,** "The Cake Boss" and *New York Times* best-selling author

Important Life Lessons from
My Special-Needs Son

LIVE LIKE SEAN

TJ Nelligan

with Theresa Foy DiGeronimo

This book is a memoir reflecting the author's present recollections of experiences over time. Its story and its words are the author's alone. Some details and characteristics may be changed, some events may be compressed, and some dialogue may be recreated.

Published by Greenleaf Book Group Press
Austin, Texas
www.gbgpress.com

Distributed by Greenleaf Book Group

For ordering information or special discounts for bulk purchases, please contact Greenleaf Book Group at PO Box 91869, Austin, TX 78709, 512.891.6100.

Design and composition by Greenleaf Book Group
Cover design by Greenleaf Book Group
Front cover photo by Michael Rosenmertz

Publisher's Cataloging-in-Publication data is available.

Print ISBN: 978-1-62634-757-1

eBook ISBN: 978-1-62634-758-8

Part of the Tree Neutral® program, which offsets the number of trees consumed in the production and printing of this book by taking proactive steps, such as planting trees in direct proportion to the number of trees used: www.treeneutral.com

Printed in the United States of America on acid-free paper

20 21 22 23 24 25 10 9 8 7 6 5 4 3 2 1

First Edition

This book is dedicated to my beautiful boy, Sean Timothy Nelligan, who passed away on Father's Day in 2019.

He taught all of those who spent time with him what unconditional love really means and so many other lessons.

Also, to all the parents and families of special-needs children who know the pain, the challenge, and the joy of loving these exceptional, phenomenal, and awesome human beings!

My hope is that these chapters will remind you of lessons your own special-needs child imparts to you and the world.

CONTENTS

ACKNOWLEDGMENTS

As I finish this labor of love—writing about my beautiful boy and all he taught us—I have so many people to thank.

First, there are the three most important people in Sean's life: his loving mother, Maggie, and his adoring sisters, Moira and Meghan. Maggie, Sean was so lucky to have you as his mother. You cared for him, protected him, and loved him like crazy. Moira and Meghan, you were Sean's idols, and he was wild about both of you. He had the two best sisters anyone could ever dream to have on their side. All four of us will miss him forever as we learn day after day that he had more to teach us about life than we could ever teach him.

Thank you to the Nelligan family, who always accepted Sean: my parents (or, as Sean knew them, Papa Tim and Grandma Helen); my siblings, Terri, Eileen, Mike, and Sheila and their spouses; Sean's cousins on both the Nelligan and McMorrow sides, who loved him. He loved all of you.

Dana Nelligan, you were there for me when Sean passed away, and you spent 11 years with me and Sean. You made our lives better because of your love for both of us. Thank you.

His friends deserve special thanks as well for giving Sean's life the joy of true friendship, especially his friend Timmy Baird, whom he knew since he was five years old at The Children's Center for Therapy and Learning for special-needs children. Bobby Fredericks was another amazing friend and teammate who worked with Sean at Nelligan Sports and at the Montville Inn for 10 years.

Sean's teachers all deserve a special thanks—especially Gail Booth at the Children's Center for Therapy and Learning (now P.G. Chambers School) and then Kathy Tauscher at the Midland School. Both of you were not only great teachers for Sean but friends of our family as well.

My friends always accepted Sean as a part of their own families and welcomed him to share in their celebrations and vacations—the Mulhalls, Vargas, Dukes, Matarazzos, Bradens, Hofferths, and so many more. Thank you.

Special Olympics New Jersey (SONJ) changed our family's lives from the time Sean was 12 and attended his first SONJ summer games through to his last days. Marc and Kathy Edenzon, you were instrumental in building Sean's confidence and in getting our entire family involved in something that opened our eyes to the capabilities, talents, and accomplishments of special-needs children. For that, I will always be grateful.

Thank you to Bob Belfiore, the head of the Law Enforcement Torch Run (LETR) for more than 35 years, and Joe Sarnoski and Larry Mays and all the men and women who participated in LETR fundraising. Their yearlong efforts raise millions of dollars for SONJ.

To every one of Sean's teammates at Special Olympics, I want you to know that he treasured and enjoyed his time with you.

Thank you to all the employees at Nelligan Sports Marketing and the Montville Inn who worked with Sean and befriended him. You were so kind, and he loved both jobs because of you.

To the people we met during our days at Nelligan Sports—coaches, athletic directors, and other employees—you all made Sean's visits to your campuses and at your games so enjoyable. I am grateful for those memories.

My co-writer, Theresa DiGeronimo: I would never have been able to write this book without your encouragement and without your motivating me to continue when I thought I was unable to go on.

My therapist, Joe Bizzaro (yes, I have a therapist and am proud of it): You encouraged me to write this book, and I would not have started it without that push.

Steve Adubato, thank you for inspiring me to write this book with your kind words after Sean's memorial and for introducing me to my incredible co-writer.

Thank you to everyone who made my son's short time on this earth enjoyable and valuable. Every one of those memories mean the world to me today and always will.

INTRODUCTION

My beloved son, Sean Timothy Nelligan, died at the age of 29 on Father's Day in 2019. As I was writing his eulogy, I noticed a recurring theme. Each time I wrote down a little story about Sean that I wanted to share with my family and friends, I found myself encouraging everyone to try to live more like him. I told the room of almost a thousand people: "Live like Sean every day and you will make the lives of others so much better, and it will make you feel better also."

Shortly after the funeral, I had golf balls imprinted with the saying "Live like Sean." I gave them to my family and golfing buddies to remind them (and myself) to be kind, be happy, be brave, be honest. To be like Sean. It became clear to me that my boy, who couldn't read or write, had tried to teach me, by his example, so many valuable life lessons. They were lessons that would vastly improve my life, if only I could learn them. It is an ongoing process. I want to live like Sean—not when it is easy, not when it is convenient, but every day. I am trying. I try each day to be more like this boy who is my hero.

This book is my attempt to share those lessons with you and to preserve the memory of an outstanding human being whose legacy is not counted in material assets but in love.

As I write, I imagine my primary readers are the family members and friends of children with special needs, and I hope that my experiences, challenges, and joys help you to find a path of hope and potential with a special-needs* child. Of course, I realize that not all special-needs children are like Sean. All children are different; some are loud, some are quiet, some are outgoing, some are shy. But the lessons from this one child have something to say to all of us. In fact, I am sure that these lessons can be useful to everyone, not just special-needs families and their constituents. This is a story about Sean, but I have no doubt that his life adventures illustrate for any reader how a family heartbreak can, in fact, be a blessing.

It took me a long time to realize that we were the perfect family for Sean. And he was the perfect child for us. Our heartbreak turned to acceptance and then joy when we learned to see the world through Sean's eyes, not our own. It is my hope that this book will do the same for you.

When I began this journey as the parent of a child with special needs, I was filled with anger, disappointment, and even rage. I wondered how I would be able to live with a child with so many issues. Now, I wonder how I will be able to live without him.

This book is my attempt to hold on to and to share with you what remains—Sean's spirit, his attitude, his love.

TJ Nelligan
Spring 2020

* There are many terms to identify those with intellectual or different abilities. I am most comfortable with the term "special-needs children" and will use that term throughout the book.

1

BE GRATEFUL

Gratitude? I didn't have much of that in my young adult life before Sean came into it. As an entrepreneur in a capitalistic society, I always wanted more. I spent my days wondering how big I could grow my company. How many more employees could I hire? When a life is built on working 10 to 12 hours a day, there isn't much time to think about gratitude.

Then Sean was born. When his mom, Maggie, and I realized that he was a "special-needs" child, I can tell you that my heart was still not filled with gratitude. I felt many emotions. Anger and fear were at the top of the list, but gratitude was nowhere to be found.

The extent of Sean's developmental issues revealed itself slowly. After his birth, we took home what appeared to be a perfect, healthy newborn. There was no indication of the trouble ahead. The first sign appeared at six months; changing his diaper, we noticed that sometimes his leg would spasm. We took him to the hospital, where the doctors said it was probably just a muscle spasm. But I knew that was not it.

I spent the night in the hospital beside his crib with a video camcorder, waiting to record a spasm. When I showed the tape to the doctor the next morning, he confirmed that Sean was having seizures. That's when the rounds of testing and doctor visits and anti-seizure medications began.

After the initial shock and hurt, I think my emotions just froze. At first, I got through each day by putting my life with Sean in a compartment called denial. I told myself: *It's going to be fine. It's going to be fine. It's going to be fine.*

THE END OF DENIAL

When Sean was about two years old and his developmental delays were becoming more alarming, a friend recommended that we see the world's top neurologist, a professor at Columbia University College of Physicians and Surgeons and a pioneer in the field of child neurology. It took a long time to get an appointment, so I was able to stay in my world of denial a bit longer. But finally, on a Saturday morning, Maggie, my mother, Sean, and I went to the doctor's home office in Englewood, New Jersey.

As we sat in the waiting room, I was silent. The doctor had already received the test results from Sean's other doctors. He knew about the seizures and had the EEG test results. Now, he wanted to talk with Sean and observe him. He watched how Sean walked, how he talked, how he reacted to various stimuli. He spent a good hour with Sean, and then it was time for the verdict.

Sean stayed in the waiting room with his grandma while Maggie and I went into the office. The doctor was behind his desk while we sat on the other side feeling frightened and insecure. I looked at all the diplomas lining the walls and the shelves of books the doctor had authored, knowing this should make me feel confident and at ease, but all I felt was scared. The fact that this man was so well respected in his field meant that I was going to have to accept what he said, and I had a sinking feeling he wasn't about to give us good news.

It was immediately clear to me that the doctor knew what he was doing. He was all about the facts. But he had no bedside manner. There was no softening the sharp edges. He had seen children like Sean many, many times in his career. It seemed that, to him, Sean was just another intellectually and developmentally damaged child. He matter-of-factly explained that Sean would never live a normal or average life. He would never fit into mainstream society. He would definitely not be able to graduate high school or go to college and, most likely, wouldn't be able to have a meaningful job.

As we left the office, I don't remember exactly what I said to the doctor in response to this news, but I'm absolutely sure it wasn't "thanks."

On the ride home, we couldn't speak. Even little Sean sat still. What words were there to accept what we had just heard? What words were there to explain how we were feeling? Those words don't exist. We were all silent.

That night, after Maggie put Sean to bed, I went into his room and shut the door behind me. I gripped the edge of the crib and looked down on my sleeping child. I asked him, "How are we going to do this?" And then I cried and cried.

ACCEPTANCE AT LAST

Sean, Grandma Helen, and Papa Tim in Beach Haven, NJ.

A MUCH-NEEDED HUG

Sean was our first grandchild. I probably made a pest of myself visiting so often, but I could just not get enough of him. When he was about two years old and still struggling to walk, my wife and I began to worry that there was something wrong with his development. We sat down with TJ and Maggie and explained our concerns. They both reacted with disbelief, and we all were feeling uncomfortable. That's when Sean jumped off his mother's lap and came across the room with his little outstretched arms to give me a big hug. I don't know for sure what he sensed, or felt, or thought, but looking back, I believe that he knew I needed a hug. And I sure did.

—Papa Tim

Finally, I had to accept that that there was a problem, and Sean *wasn't* going to be okay. I couldn't keep Sean in a neat little compartment in my mind anymore. There would be no more "work goes here, marriage goes here, Sean goes here."

That was when I felt the true burden of disappointment. Getting this news about Sean shattered my expectations. It was the death of my dreams for my first child. My son. Sean would not be the starting pitcher for his baseball team. He would not play a musical instrument in the school band. He would not get married and have children of his own. The Nelligan name would not move on through him to the next generation. He would not live a life that I thought he deserved. My heart was broken. What did I have to be thankful for?

Although no parent wants a child to have a difficult life, and many of my feelings were rooted in this worry about what would happen to Sean, I admit that some of my emotions were coming from my fear about how he was going to negatively impact *my* future. Raising a child with multiple disabilities sets the parents on a long, winding journey with no road map or even a clear destination. There are years and years ahead of nonstop visits to doctors, speech therapists, occupational therapists, and physical therapists. Then there are tests, evaluations, hospitalizations, medications. And so much more. I don't remember even once thinking "thank you."

I realize now that gratitude is the foundation of happiness. The two go together. And perhaps that is why in the first decade of Sean's life, I had neither. I was too busy protecting him. In doing so, I'm sure I lost many opportunities to enjoy him and thank God for him, but at that point I couldn't do anything else. It was like carrying around an egg that could drop and break at any wrong turn. His mom and I felt that we needed to protect him from getting hurt—physically and emotionally. We wanted to protect him from hurting himself, not only when he stumbled, which was often, but also from people who might say mean things to him, from an educational establishment that didn't understand his needs, from a world where he wasn't "normal."

This was going to be a hard and long road—for me. At that time, I couldn't see that the shattered dreams were not Sean's dreams. He was not angry or disappointed. He seemed quite happy to be alive. Every day was a great day. Going through the thousands of pictures of Sean while preparing for his memorial, his sister Meghan noticed that he wore his wide and wonderful smile in every single photo. (Well, except for the one in which his sister Moira is using him to practice her hair-cutting skills.) He always carried himself through each day with joy and, yes, with a sense of gratitude that astounded and confused me.

I felt confused, probably because I never really knew what gratitude meant until Sean taught it to me. That is ironic because I'm sure that people who didn't know Sean would look at him and think, "What does he have to be thankful for?" However, his sense of gratitude wasn't the result of an easy, protected life—not at all. Sean suffered emotionally and physically through those early years: the years of physical therapy, when he was learning to walk with leg braces that hurt so much. The years of speech therapy, when he lived with the frustration of wanting to communicate but being unable to form words or write letters. The years of confusion, when he seemed to be hesitant to be involved in the world around him.

Aunt Sheila cheering Sean on at the 2014 Special Olympics USA Games.

LIFE IN PERSPECTIVE

Sean always greeted me with a smile and a willingness to play and laugh. Seeing Sean always kept life in perspective.

—Aunt Sheila Nelligan Himes

A CHANGE OF PERSPECTIVE

Despite his struggles, Sean was able to have so many of the things we all want to have and should take the time to be grateful for: kind and helpful teachers, good friends, loving sisters, a supportive family, a passion for sports and music. Those things filled Sean's heart with happiness, and his ability to truly appreciate the important things in life showed me how my own lack of gratitude for these same things made happiness impossible.

I couldn't feel grateful because I believed that I was somehow entitled to a "normal" child. But Sean didn't feel this way, so his gratitude came easily. It wasn't until years later that I saw in his happiness and his acceptance of the life he had been given that the neurologist was 100 percent right. Sean was never going to be average. He was exceptional.

Sean stood tall and rose above the doctor's dire predictions because he never felt gypped. He didn't feel that he was missing out on anything. He had no expectations or sense of entitlement. From his perspective, he wasn't cheated by life or given less than anyone else. In fact, he seemed to know that he was given more than most of us will ever have. He entered every room with his signature smile, making everyone he met feel special. He didn't apologize for himself. He didn't want to hide so no one would know he was "different." As he grew into his teens, Sean walked around like he was the mayor, saying hello to everyone, giving out hugs, handshakes, and compliments: "I like your new haircut." "Those are nice shoes." "You are a good friend." He would say these things with a confidence that was unimaginable a decade earlier. He showed his gratitude for everything in life by living that life with joy, contentment, and acceptance. And I was learning to do the same.

Live Like Sean

I have begun this book with a lesson about gratitude because, in my experience, it is the hardest lesson to learn. It takes the longest to learn. And yet it is the most enduring lesson and is now the foundation of my happiness. I am truly grateful for every memory—the painful and the joyful—that highlights Sean's relentless efforts to show me a way through my own heartbreak and to have gratitude for our life together.

I realize that each special-needs child is unique, just as all children are. Some are naturally happy; some are not. Some are outgoing; some are not. And so on. Therefore I don't pretend that just because Sean was able to wake each day with an attitude of gratitude that this is the case for all children. However, I do believe that all special-needs children offer us the opportunity to see the world with new eyes—their eyes. It is the world in which they live; they know no other. For Sean, that gratitude grew out of his ability to live a happy and meaningful life with his family and friends (and to see the Giants win the Super Bowl).

For me, learning how to be grateful didn't happen like a bolt of lightning. I had to absorb that lesson over time. Learning to live like Sean started when I slowly began to see the world from his point of view, rather than through my own lens of disappointment.

If you are a family member of a special-needs child, I don't expect that after reading this you will suddenly feel grateful. But there are some things you can begin to do:

- Give yourself the chance to actively and consciously look for moments to say "thank you."
- Let those small moments contribute to growing the hope for future happiness.

I hope that together, we can move through each of the upcoming chapters from a place of despair to a place touched by gratitude.

I can finally answer the question that I had asked a million times: Why would God give me this child? Twenty-nine years later, I know the answer. I had a lot to learn about living a good life built on a foundation of gratitude, and I needed Sean to teach me. For this gift, I am forever grateful.

2

BE PRESENT

I'm a handshaker, a backslapper, a networker. I can work a room. I can also multitask—making a business deal while playing a round of golf, while checking my email, while texting my friends, while exploring a new restaurant, while buying a pair of shoes. That's what I do. But it's not what I want to do anymore. More often, I want to live like Sean and be present in the moment, giving the person I am with and the activity I'm engaged in my full attention. If I can do this even just once a day, Sean will live on in me.

HOW MANY HOURS HAVE I WASTED?

I know it's trendy these days to "be present." The top results of a quick Google search for this term illustrate its popularity: "35 Exercises & Tools to Live in the Present Moment," "Six Steps to Living in the Moment," "10 Tips to Start Living in the Present," "10 Mindfulness Exercises for Living in the Present Moment," and on and on. And on. Sean didn't need exercises or tips or tools to be present. He just naturally knew how to live in the moment better than any self-help guru.

One reason he could do this so well was because he was focused on the now. What a gift! So often during the course of the day, I catch myself thinking about decisions I made yesterday or last week or even years ago. I think about how different things might be if I could have a "do over." I spend hours of my life thinking this way, even though I know I can't change the past and I can't undo the consequences of those past decisions. How many hours of my life have been wasted by looking back instead of looking at the moment I'm in?

I'm no better when it comes to looking ahead. I obsess over what I will be doing tomorrow, next week, and next year. Of course, it's good to set a goal and have a plan for the long run, but I spend so much time thinking and worrying about the next step that I totally lose track of this moment. Of the person I'm with and the activity I'm engaged in. This moment is the one and only thing I have complete control over, and yet I waste the opportunity to give it my full attention. No more. I want to live in the moment like Sean as much as I possibly can.

Sean with TJ's brother, Uncle Mike.

ENJOYING THE MOMENT

All we have is right now. This moment. Tomorrow is not promised. Sean had a special gift for enjoying this moment, whether it was running errands with Dad, taking a picture with his uncle, or whatever. Whatever he was doing, he did it with a smile on his face and love in his heart. I did not get to experience enough of these moments in person, but through the magic of Facebook, I got to watch his ever-present smile in everything he was doing.

—Uncle Mike Nelligan

FULL AND UNDIVIDED ATTENTION

Sean lived not for today but for the moment. In that moment, he gave the person and the activity his full attention, and I have no doubt it was this skill that gave such strength to all his relationships. Whomever he was with at that exact moment in time had his full and undivided attention. I felt Sean's power of being present at every Yankees and Giants game we attended together. He didn't miss one pitch or one play by fiddling with his phone or by strolling the indoor concessions for food. He was fully committed to each moment in the game. He shared his excitement with me and me alone each time Aaron Judge hit a homer or Eli Manning threw a touchdown. He didn't spend time looking around to see who else might be in the crowd. He didn't take his eye off the game to post to Instagram. He was there to enjoy the game with his dad, and from beginning to end he made me feel like I was the only one who mattered to him. (Of course, Sean would have high fives for everyone within arm's reach when his team made a great play.)

Sean and Coach Geri Fredericks, Bobby's mom, both passed away within months of each other.

YOU NEVER KNOW

If there's anything that I've learned from being around Sean since 2010, it's that you always have to try to have some fun, no matter what it is that you're doing or how bored you are. You never know when it's going to be your turn to leave and join everyone who has left us (like my mom, my first Special Olympics coach) in heaven.

—Bobby Fredericks

A NEAR MISS OF AN ICONIC MOMENT

One very memorable event—captured live only because of Sean's insistence on staying focused in the moment—was Derek Jeter's last home game of his career at Yankee Stadium on September 25, 2014. I remember every detail: The temperature that night was 61 degrees, and the sky was overcast as we took our seats behind home plate. Sean was wearing his Jeter number 2 jersey and his classic blue Yankees hat.

We had watched Jeter, the Babe Ruth of our generation, through many years, many games, and many amazing moments, all of which added up to his being a 14-time All-Star and five-time World Series champion. Sean and I were both excited to be present at Jeter's last game. I remember vividly how thrilled Sean was as the Yankees cruised into the ninth inning with a 5–2 lead. However, as exciting as the game was, I assumed it was won, and I wanted to leave to beat the traffic and crowd. But Sean wasn't having any of that. He wasn't thinking about what's next; he was at this exciting game now, and he was not leaving. And if it weren't for his insistence on staying present, we would have missed the most iconic moment in Jeter's career—maybe in any athlete's career.

In the top of the ninth inning, the Orioles scored three runs to tie the game at 5–5. Now the Yankees' win was not so guaranteed. In the bottom of the inning, Jeter was up third with men on base and a chance to win this final game for his team. Sean joined the 48,613 fans chanting "Der-ek Jet-er," stopping only to tell me with full confidence, "The Yankees are going to win with a walk-off from Derek."

When the 86-mph changeup hit Jeter's bat and the ball flew between first and second base, allowing pinch runner Antoan Richardson to beat the throw home, Jeter threw his hands up into the air as he rounded first base. The crowd's response was right out of a

Hollywood movie. The place erupted in thunderous noise. I thought people were going to be jumping off the upper deck. You could feel the stadium actually moving. It was crazy.

There are many iconic photos of Jeter jumping for joy then, but I still think it's possible that Sean's happiness was even greater. He was screaming. Smiling. Clapping. And also jumping for joy. In that moment, he was all in—with every ounce of his being. I got to share that moment with him only because he made us stay. Me? I had been thinking ahead, thinking about traffic, thinking about the other things I had yet to do that evening. I would have been in an Uber on the way home, and I would have missed one of the greatest moments in Yankees history, which, however, comes second to sharing one of the greatest moments in my son's life.

By the way, Sean's correct prediction that Jeter would win the game with a walk-off hit wasn't as surprising at it might seem. He said the same thing about every Yankees player in that situation. Every once in a while, he was right!

The Nelligans—one big, accepting family.

THE GIFT OF BEING PRESENT

Of all Sean's wonderful traits, the one that I try to emulate every day is his ability to be present and focused on whomever he was with. He really knew how to give the gift of his presence! He made everyone feel like they were the most important person in the room. He gave his full and undivided attention and filled the heart of anyone who spent time with him. He always listened; he never passed judgment; he smiled. I hope I can make him proud by living like him when I am with others.

—Aunt Sheila Nelligan Himes

MAKING ONE SPECIAL PERSON FEEL SPECIAL

This special way of living in the moment was not something Sean reserved just for me (or Derek Jeter). Everyone got the same attention when the moment called for it. Every summer his grandparents Helen and Tim would visit us at our beach house at the Jersey Shore. Sean knew that would be his special time with Grandma. They'd always go to lunch and to the Surflight Theater in Beach Haven. No one else was invited. No one else could go with them. This was his time to be with this one special person. Of course, I would tease him and ask if Grandpa and I could come also. He always replied, "Nope, just Grandma and me are going." Sean didn't want anyone to take his attention away from that person and that event.

I don't know what happened in detail on his lunch/theater dates with his grandma because I was never there, but I know enough. After they returned, Sean would tell everyone that it was the best show ever and that he and Grandma had a blast. He would tell us what Grandma said and what Grandma did and what parts of the play were her favorites. He was obviously fully invested in that relationship for those three to four hours.

Sean being present with Grandma Helen while looking at the ocean in Beach Haven, NJ.

A WONDERFUL TIME TOGETHER

My greatest memories of Sean from early on was our yearly dinner-and-show outing. Sean would tell everyone that only he and Grandma could go. He loved telling Papa and TJ that they couldn't go. The outing began when he was about 18 years old. We started going to the children's theater after a dinner at a restaurant that he liked and where he could order whatever he wanted. He also really enjoyed the show, because he had a very good sense of music and story line. He was also developing social skills that showed in his smile and his gratitude for a fun and enjoyable night. As the ritual developed over the years, he would always remind me of what we do and how we do it. His desire to make our time together wonderful for me was his prime goal.

—Grandma Helen

Live Like Sean

I tend to scatter my attention. In the past, if someone wanted to join me when I planned to have lunch with someone else, I'd say, "Sure! The more the merrier!" No more. Sean showed me that if I plan to spend time with one person, I should give that person my full attention.

He applied the same focus to his friends. When friends would visit, he would play board games with some and talk sports with others.

But he always had one-on-one conversations with each person, one at a time. He seemed to know that this was important to whomever he was with and that he had a special and different relationship with each friend, cousin, aunt, and uncle. Every one of them has stories about their one-on-one moments with Sean and how during that time together, they felt his love for them. And they returned that love.

This special-needs child and the young man he became seemed to have the secret for living in the moment. Why is it so hard for us to learn this lesson? Why do we complicate our lives with unnecessary distractions that rob us of the power of living in the moment? I want my family and friends to feel that powerful connection with me after we have spent time together. There are lessons from Sean that will help us to do that.

- Be attentive to the moment you're in by putting aside cell phones and other devices, and letting thoughts of future projects or problems drift away. Fully take part in whatever activity you're participating in.
- Engage with the person you're with, one-on-one, as though you have a special relationship with them. You do.

This is the beautiful lesson of being present that Sean tried to teach everyone who ever met him—if they were attentive enough to notice.

3

BE FRIENDLY

I'm outgoing. I'm gregarious. I'm at ease in a crowd. And I always considered myself exceptionally friendly. Then Sean showed me that I have a lot to learn.

Being outgoing doesn't make me friendly. The two are not at all the same thing. When I work the room at a social event, giving everyone a quick "Nice to see you," I am not being genuinely friendly. "Genuine" describes the aspect of Sean's friendliness that set him apart. His friendliness wasn't fake, contrived, or self-serving. When he entered a room, he worked it like a celebrity, but not with quick, shallow greetings. He stopped and talked and made each person feel special.

A FINAL GOODBYE

Sean's ability to make a genuine connection is most vivid in my mind when I think back to the last big party he attended on the Friday night before he passed away. Ironically, it was a goodbye party. The sale of the Montville Inn, the restaurant in Montville, New Jersey, that I owned and where Sean worked, would be finalized in the coming week. That Friday night friends all stopped by to reminisce and wish us good luck.

The restaurant business is tough. It's built on a terrible business model in which you pour hundreds of thousands of dollars into the enterprise and then find that its success depends on sometimes unexpected occurrences, like a 16-year-old hostess who has to leave early to study for an algebra test she has in the morning. But I loved the business, nevertheless.

The inn had been built by Dutch settlers in 1770 and had gone through several renovations before I bought it, knocked down the original structure, and put up an old-fashioned colonial inn with a large wraparound porch, a copper bar, two private dining rooms, and a main dining area. The décor focused on the history of Montville and surrounding towns with pictures of historic buildings, the local railroad station, the Morris Canal, O'Dowd's Dairy, the old Montville hotel, and the like.

My own relationship with the Montville Inn goes back to high school, when it was more of a biker bar and, as underage kids, we'd send in the tallest of the gang to get take-out beers. Now I was the owner saying goodbye to more than a decade of good memories.

That night we were in the tavern portion of the inn with about 100 people, mostly friends and long-time customers. Good friends like the Dukes, the Matarazzos, the Bradens, the Vargas, the Mulhalls, and many others came to celebrate our 11-year run at the Inn and all the wonderful recollections the place held—the communion parties, graduation parties, the important lifetime events that happened there.

From the minute he arrived, Sean walked around the inn like—well, like he owned the place. Sean and his good friend Bobby Fredericks had worked there for nine years. They put inventory away in the fridge and on the shelves. They broke down boxes. They cut the potatoes into french fries. They did food prep. They cleaned the tables and windows and swept the porch. This was a real job for them with real colleagues who knew how hard they worked and who treated them with kindness and respect. The job was a source of great pride for these boys, and it was hard for them to give it up. For Sean, the night was a sad occasion because he would miss the job, but it was also a happy opportunity to celebrate past good times with lots of good people.

Two days later Sean had a seizure and passed away peacefully in his sleep.

After Sean's death, I was unbelievably touched by the number of people who sent me selfies that were taken that night showing Sean with his trademark smile and with an arm around those he loved so much.

One interaction in particular epitomized how Sean embraced people he knew. Family friends Deb and Brian Mulhall were among those at the party. Sean had seen Brian recently in Florida when we went fishing, but he hadn't seen Deb for three years. No matter, when the couple walked in the door, Sean was the first one to run over and greet her warmly. Later that night, she told me, with a teary smile, "I thought Sean wouldn't remember me, but he came up to me and said, 'Hi Deb'—and almost tackled me with a big hug. I was so happy!"

Brian and Deb knew that time can sometimes erase good memories, but that fact never occurred to Sean. He never hesitated, held back, or worried that he might give a hearty, loud, loving greeting to someone who didn't remember him. Granted, it's hard to forget Sean, but still, Sean didn't know that. He just felt that if he remembered a person, he had a reason to say hello.

I think most of us have been in situations where we worry about feeling embarrassed if we say hello to someone who doesn't recognize us. Sometimes we pretend we don't remember them and don't say hello, avoiding the risk. But an opportunity to reconnect is lost. Why? What is the worst thing that can happen? I know Sean would be quick to remind the person drawing a blank who he was and then he'd pick up the relationship without a moment of embarrassment. Sean's friendliness made others feel good, feel special, feel loved. I want to be more like Sean.

MAKE ANY MOMENT A MEMORY

Sean was great at making any interaction memorable. When I think back on the 2014 Special Olympics USA Games, there are so many remarkable memories. The opening ceremony had powerful speakers and performers. I got to meet and take a selfie with a supermodel and a *Sports Illustrated* cover model. I met multiple television and movie personalities. I watched my brother give an amazing speech in front of 20,000 adoring fans. But my favorite memory is of Sean asking me to take a picture with him.

It was a simple gesture in the middle of a hectic day, but it meant—and still means—the world to me. He was able to slow the pace for 10 seconds and create a moment that stood out over all the other unforgettable moments of a great week.

—Uncle Mike Nelligan

Making time on a busy day to pose with Uncle Mike.

TURNING STRANGERS INTO FRIENDS

When I take my seat on a plane and sit in silence for two hours without once speaking to the person sitting two inches away from me, I am not being friendly, and I know it. Sometimes, I don't want to be friendly. I want to get some work done, or I just want to rest. But sometimes I isolate myself out of habit and plug unthinkingly into a Netflix movie on my laptop. In situations like that, I want the memory of Sean to nudge me into friendliness.

If Sean were sitting in that seat, he wouldn't hold back, worried that he might be rebuffed, or be intruding, or be embarrassed. He would just smile and say hi. If the person didn't respond in a kind way, he would back off. But it's remarkable to see how most people *do* want to engage in conversation if someone else starts it. Before long, Sean would know more about that person than their next-door neighbor.

I kept this in mind when I was sitting in a coffee shop today, my earbuds plugged in and my eyes focused on my phone. I definitely was not being friendly. Sean never used technology to distract or distance himself from the people who surrounded him—even random people. Using earbuds is often an intentional way to isolate ourselves from the intrusion of others. After all, if I can't hear you, you can't bother me. Sometimes, that's the plan. But other times it's just a habit that separates me from the world around me, and that's not how I want to live.

On the occasions I've tried being friendly with strangers, inevitably, it turns out that we have something in common. Often we know the same people; at the very least, we end up smiling. Recently, I was waiting to board a plane in Florida and saw a young girl with Down syndrome sitting silently. No one acknowledged her at all for about a half hour. When it was time to line up, I ended up behind her and her parents. Channeling Sean, I started up a conversation with this little girl.

"So, what did you do during your visit here?" I asked. She turned to me and with the biggest smile answered loudly, "I was swimming with a dolphin!" She then told me every detail of this amazing experience. She had been quiet the entire time she was in the airport and now was bursting with excitement. I loved listening to her and was disappointed with myself for waiting so long to say hello.

In Sean's beautiful life, I saw very clearly that connecting with another person, even a stranger, enriches the moment and is far better than sitting in silence next to another human being.

THE MAGIC OF FEELING SPECIAL

I always felt really proud about my relationship with Sean—and a little guilty, because I felt he and I were closer than some of his other relatives. Sean and I would see each other at family holidays and fall back into easy conversations about whatever we were talking about the last time we were together. How naïve was I? It's only now that I realize he made everyone feel the same way! That "magic" that I had with Sean was really the essence of who he was. I'm so damn lucky to have had those times with Sean and am working toward living more like him.

—Uncle John Himes

Uncle John Himes and cousin Jack Himes are proud members of "Team Sean."

PAUPER OR KING

In 2003 our family gathered together in St. Thomas, in the U.S. Virgin Islands, to celebrate the Thanksgiving holiday. Although when he hit his late teens, Sean could sleep all morning, at the age of 13, he still woke at 5 a.m. every day. On this particular morning, I got up with him, and we went off to find a bagel and some juice.

Then we went to the lounge chairs surrounding the outdoor pool to enjoy our breakfast. The pool sat high on the property, overlooking the shimmering Caribbean Sea. Except for one early morning swimmer doing laps in the clear blue pool water, we were the only guests around.

I took a moment to take in the view, the beauty of the morning, and the rare opportunity to just sit and relax; I had not really looked at the person in the water until he swam up to the steps to exit the pool. Sean, however, had apparently zeroed in on the swimmer right from the start. It was typical of Sean to put his focus on people, rather than his environment. When he called out, "You're a good swimmer!" I turned my attention to the man in the pool and noticed that the swimmer had no legs and only one arm and that his face looked familiar. Then it registered. The man was Max Cleland, a senator from Georgia and a U.S. Army veteran of the Vietnam War, who had earned the Silver Star and the Bronze Star.

"Thanks, buddy," he said.

Sean and Cleland talked about who-knows-what for about five minutes, and then Sean turned to me and, remembering his manners, said, "Oh, Max, this is my dad, TJ." Until that point, I hadn't been a part of their conversation.

"Nice to meet you, Senator," I said.

Yes, I knew we were meeting an admired war hero and elected official, but Sean was simply talking to someone who was in the pool near where he happened to be having breakfast. That's all he needed to know to strike up a conversation that showed genuine interest in that person's life.

Then I heard Sean ask, "Max, what happened to your legs?" This is the kind of question that you and I might cringe at, but to Sean it was an obvious question if you wanted to get to know this guy.

"They got blown up in the war, Sean."

"I'm sorry, Max."

"War is a bad thing," said the senator, looking directly into Sean's eyes.

No doubt Cleland realized that Sean had special needs, and although the senator clearly did not need help, I'm sure his next move was intended to make Sean feel important. And it did.

"Sean," he asked, "would you wheel me up to the elevator?"

The two went off like old buddies.

If I had been at that pool alone, I would not have interrupted the senator's swim nor bothered him with a hello when he finished. And I certainly wouldn't have asked him what happened to his legs. But why not? If I've learned anything from Sean, it's that a simple hello is never intrusive or bothersome. If a person isn't interested in continuing a conversation, they'll just cut it off. No big deal.

As that day went on, I forgot all about seeing Max Cleland at the pool and never mentioned it to anyone in the family. Later that night, as our entire extended family was standing in the hotel lobby waiting for a cab to take us to a restaurant, I noticed Cleland being wheeled across the lobby. Seeing Sean, he directed his aide to bring him over to us. When my dad saw Cleland approaching, he whispered to me, "Isn't that the senator from Georgia?"

"Yup," I said. I knew what was coming next.

"Hey, Sean," Cleland said. "Where you goin', buddy?"

"We're going to dinner. Max, this is my Papa Tim, my grandma, my mom, my dad, and my sisters."

"Nice to meet you all and to see my buddy again."

Everyone was speechless as they mumbled confused hellos. No one else in our family, or in the hotel for that matter, was chatting with the senator—just Sean.

"Now I've seen everything," said my dad. But there was more to come.

As we turned from the senator, we saw that the line for a taxi had grown longer. Within seconds, one of the car valets saw us and came over.

"Sean! Where you going? Who are you with?"

"I'm going to dinner," said Sean, "with my whole family."

"How many?"

"I don't know. All of them," he said sweeping his arms toward us.

"Hey, John," said the valet, "two van cabs on the side for Sean. Now."

We were treated like celebrities because of Sean. My father got it right when he said, "This is a special-needs guy? He's the most connected, powerful person in the family."

Why? Simply because he was genuinely friendly. When Sean connected with people, he made them feel like they were important to him. He understood that every connection is an opportunity to make a positive impact on someone's day.

The reaction to Sean from both Senator Cleland and the valet points to another important aspect of Sean's friendliness. He made no distinction between knowing the senator and knowing the valet. Both connections had equal value in his eyes.

I learned this, to my great embarrassment, in 2011 when Sean was 21 years old and began working for Nelligan Sports Marketing. Along with his friend Bobby Fredericks, Sean came every Monday to work on accounts receivable: They would fold the bills, put them in envelopes, run them through the postage machine, and mail them off. The first day on the job, his mom dropped Sean off, and he came in happy and ready to get to work. At the end of the day, as we were leaving the building, Sean stopped at the front desk where a large security guard was sitting.

"Hey, Bruno. I'll see you next week."

What? Sean had worked at my office only one day and somehow he knew the security guard's name? I'd walked past the man for 10 years, giving a little wave, but with so much on my mind—what I had to get done, who I had to call—that I never stopped to ask his name. Sean not only knew his name, he knew something about the man. "Say hello to your granddaughters for me," Sean added.

I watched this exchange feeling about two inches tall.

"Hi, Bruno," I said. "I'm TJ Nelligan."

"Yeah, I know," said Bruno. "Your office is on the seventh floor."

As we walked to the car to go home, I asked Sean how he knew Bruno.

"Oh," he said. "This morning when I came in with Mom, I met him. I told Bruno it's my first day of work. He is so nice, and he has two granddaughters. He really loves them, you know."

Unbelievable. In the 10 years that I'd been walking past that desk at least twice a day, why had I never had such a friendly exchange?

LIKE A MAGNET

Sean was a magnet. Everyone was attracted to him because, without trying, he made others feel good. At every Nelligan gathering, everyone would vie to be next to Sean, to spend time with Sean, to speak with him, dance with him, and get a selfie with him. Everyone wanted to laugh and joke around with him, to hug him and tell him how much he is loved. Sean inevitably would turn the tables and ask how we were doing and joke with us and laugh at our attempts to be funny, and, of course, to share a big hug. The thing is that Sean did all that so much better than any of us could. He didn't expect or demand attention. He was charismatic and a giver and, in turn, attracted the attention he so rightly deserved. Sean came by these traits naturally, and they were enhanced by being in an environment that included others who cared deeply for him and others with special needs.

—Aunt Terri Nelligan

The Nelligan clan sporting their "Team Sean" t-shirts.

Live Like Sean

To Sean, being friendly was the same as breathing. It came naturally. It was not a social obligation. It was an extension of who he was inside—a sincerely kind person who cared about the lives of others. When Sean asked, "How are you?" he actually wanted to know the answer.

I understand that trying to be genuinely friendly can make some people feel uncomfortable. It's much easier to walk past the doormen, the desk clerks, the security guards, and other strangers with a quick "Good morning." If you try to strike up a more genuine conversation, it might feel awkward and even contrived.

Even with those we know, our internal dialogue sometimes goes like this: *I can't remember his name. He probably won't remember me. It's been such a long time, what's the point? I don't want to bother her. I'm in a hurry.*

Sean had none of these concerns.

What I've learned from trying to be more like Sean is that if you look for moments to connect with others in a sincere way, eventually the interaction becomes a genuine expression of interest and kindness. It enriches the moment and ultimately the quality of your life.

What can we do to start making these connections?

- Begin by shedding inhibitions. *Don't worry about feeling awkward or shy.*
- Be genuinely friendly.
- Share a smile, a hello, and a short but sincere conversation with neighbors, colleagues, forgotten friends, strangers, kings, and paupers alike.

Before you know it, you'll be living like Sean.

4

BE A GOOD FRIEND

Being a good friend is different from being friendly. Yes, Sean was an exceptionally friendly person, as is obvious from the previous chapter, but that is not the same thing as being a good friend. Friendship is a special relationship between two people that is long term and steady.

When asked what makes a good friend, you might answer that it is someone who can be counted on to come to the rescue. Someone who you can call in the middle of the night to cry or vent. Someone who will help you move (for the fifth time!) without complaint. And so on.

But Sean couldn't do any of these things, and yet, I believe he knew more about how to be a good friend than most people I've ever met. In fact, after his death, many classmates and teammates wrote the exact same phrase on his Facebook page: "He was my good friend." And they all meant it.

Sean's friendships flipped the script. He based his close relationships on what he could give to the other person, expecting nothing in return. He was not someone's friend because of what they could do for him, or what they could get him, or who they could introduce him to. He placed no demands on his friends, no expectations. And he would never exploit a friend for personal gain. He had no ulterior motives. The classmates and teammates who befriended him knew he could not come to their rescue, or open doors for their ambitions, or pull them out of a jam. But they knew he would always be supportive, encouraging, loyal, honest, accepting, and forgiving. And that makes a good friend.

Sean, Timmy Baird, and Bobby Fredericks after a Storm game.

BEST FRIENDS

Sean had many good friends. But he had two best friends—Timmy Baird and Bobby Fredericks. His connection with these two beautiful boys was everything a true friendship should be. It embodies everything I now want to bring to my friendships.

—TJ Nelligan

Sean's sincere and loving relationship with his friends stripped away the pretenses and self-serving motives that too often masquerade as friendship. Sean's uniquely genuine form of friendship is one that we can all learn from.

A GOOD FRIEND IS SUPPORTIVE AND ENCOURAGING

Of course, we expect to emotionally support a friend, and we expect that friend to support us in return. But what does the word "support" really mean? For one thing, where Sean was concerned, it meant that he could never play defense on the basketball court.

I first saw Sean's definition of a supportive friendship in action when he was about 16 years old. I stopped by his school while he was in gym class playing basketball. He was the tallest kid in the class at the time, which gave him an obvious advantage in this sport that he loved. When I peeked in to watch, he was running down the court on defense, covering a player dribbling the ball to the basket. As his classmate went to take his shot, Sean could have easily swatted the ball away. Instead, he moved out of the way, watched the boy make the basket, and then ran up to him saying, "Good shot!" I later tried to explain that his job on defense was to block the shot and make sure the ball *didn't* go into the basket. He looked at me with confusion and then confidently informed me, "That's not nice."

Basketball was Sean's favorite sport, and he knew how the game was played, but, to him, supporting and encouraging the efforts and accomplishments of others was more important than blocking a shot or scoring a point.

As Sean grew older, he played basketball for a Special Olympics team called Storm. By that time, his coaches were aware that Sean was too kind to play defense. Instead he used his strong jump shot to help his team score points on offense. He loved making baskets, but whether he scored 20 points in a game (which, shockingly, he did once) or he made just one basket was irrelevant to him. For him, the game was all about being a teammate and friend. So even on offense, he gave away points. When a teammate scored a basket, Sean would run to the player to give a high five—while the other team ran by him on a fast break to score. He could care less; his friend had just done something great and deserved his attention and encouragement.

That genuine enjoyment of his friends' accomplishments was also always evident when Sean was on the sidelines. If he was on the bench, he never once seemed to mind the loss of playing time. He was happy that his teammates all got a chance to enjoy the game and would loudly cheer them on. If someone missed a basket, Sean would never show disappointment or shout something hurtful. "That's okay!" he'd yell. "You'll get the next one." That's what a friend needs to hear, and that's what you could count on from Sean.

Endurance racer Robyn Benincasa has been quoted as saying, "You don't inspire your teammates by showing them how amazing you are. You inspire them by showing them how amazing they are." Benincasa offers this insight as a trained athlete, best-selling author, and motivational speaker; Sean knew this truth in his heart and lived it every day on the basketball court and in life. He loved the camaraderie of sports and the friendships that the game gave him far more than the actual competition. With his high fives and "good job!" his teammates knew Sean was their biggest supporter. This was evident at his memorial when they showed up in their Special Olympics Storm uniforms to show their friend their respect.

I realize that emulating Sean's attitude in a sports arena is not a good idea. Most athletes play to win. But practicing that kind of support in life situations is a goal we all can strive for.

Storm teammates congratulate Sean after his first-ever soccer goal.

CHEERING FOR A CHAMPION

When Sean scored his first goal in one of our Special Olympics soccer games, everyone from our team ran over to Sean as if we had just won the championship, which was still a few weeks away. Sean was always cheering on his teammates, and now we were so happy for him. I also remember how Sean and I would feed each other the ball, whether it was soccer or basketball. If I fed Sean the ball, the chances were that our team was going to score; if Sean didn't have the shot, he would pass the ball to someone who did!

—Best friend and coworker Bobby Fredericks

A GOOD FRIEND IS BOTH HONEST AND ACCEPTING

Other than occasionally taking four cookies when he knew he was allowed only one, Sean was brutally honest. He didn't know how to deceive someone, and he expected the same kind of honesty from those he called his friends. If he liked your shoes, he'd say so, and if he didn't, it's likely you'd hear about that, too. If his friend didn't love the Giants football team as much as he did, he would tease about a lack of judgment, but he would never hold someone's beliefs or opinions against them. If you were his friend, you could count on him to tell you the truth, and you could always share your own truth right back at him.

This innate honesty was a kind of friendship detector. Although Sean was friendly, he chose his friends carefully. Part of his selection criteria was a person's genuineness. It was crucial to put aside all pretense and be honest about who you are and what you believe.

Too often in my own friendships, I've seen people try to change or hide who they really are so their friends will accept them. It's a common response. Before sitting down at a social event, we may mentally run through reminders: *When you're talking to Susie, don't mention Trump. If you sit next to Anthony, don't say anything about feminists.* Why do we do that? Why is it when we're with people we call friends, we find it difficult to express our beliefs and share our thoughts? Why can't we be accepted for who we are and for what we believe? Because we don't live like Sean.

No one would dare tell Sean what he could and could not talk about with someone. If so-and-so didn't like his opinion, so-and-so could just walk away. Sean didn't consider it his problem. For his part, he was smart enough to surround himself only with those whom he liked and trusted and who would accept him as is. Those people he loved unconditionally, and they loved him back.

Occasionally, Sean would talk with an associate of mine briefly and then tell me later, "He's not nice." Sensing what was in people's hearts, he would be honest about his willingness—or unwillingness—to have future interactions. In the same way, if you were his friend, you were his friend. I always found it interesting that my daughters would introduce a friend of mine to their own friends by saying, "This is my father's friend Bill." But Sean knew no degrees of separation, and his introduction would reflect that: "This is my friend Bill," he'd say.

Sean and Grandma Helen at the 2014 Special Olympics USA Games, where Sean would win a gold and a silver medal in the bocce competition.

WITHOUT JUDGMENT

Sean had so many talents, but the best was his ability to accept everyone without judgment. He accepted everyone where they were. But by no means did he develop that skill without being wary of anyone who was not very kind. He shied away from those he did not trust.

—Grandma Helen

A GOOD FRIEND IS LOYAL

It goes without saying that the words "friendship" and "loyalty" go together. But I'm stating it here because the connection between the two words is often miserably weak when compared with the kind of loyalty Sean brought to his friendships.

Remember, if you were Sean's friend, you were his friend—directly, intensely, and always. If he heard anyone (even someone who was a good friend) say something negative about one of his other friends, he did not hold back. He would not join in the negative conversation, and he also would not sit by quietly. I've heard him stand up and say, "Stop. That's not nice. That's my friend." And that was the end of it. In Sean's world, to be a loyal friend meant being willing to stand up for that friend at the risk of reprimanding another person, even someone close to you.

THE SUPPORT OF TRUE FRIENDS

On that awful Father's Day morning that Sean died in Long Beach Island, New Jersey, other friends jumped into action to remind me what true friendship looks like. I have no idea who told them the news, but very quickly Nick Matarazzo, Andy Duke, and Brian Mulhall were at my side. They gave up their own Father's Day celebrations to be with me and to drive me north back to Hoboken. Sean was responsible for my finding the support through friendship that I would need without him by my side.

—TJ Nelligan

There is another form of loyalty that Sean brought to his friendships. That was the loyalty of being completely present in the moment with his friends and not splitting his attention with anyone or anything else. His connections were always one-on-one, in person, and direct. There was no Snapchat, no texting, no emailing to get in the way.

I saw this in action at family gatherings, at big sporting events, at his school, at work—anywhere Sean was in the company of people he considered his friends. One example was when we were at a Taylor Swift concert with a group of his friends. I am absolutely sure that many people at that concert were ignoring their companions and instead were looking around to see who else was in attendance, who was wearing a better outfit, who could make useful introductions. But Sean spent every second directly connected with his friends—laughing, dancing, waving signs, and sharing his infectious joy with everyone he loved.

Being a good friend like Sean is not easy. I'm as guilty as the next guy of splitting my attention. If I sit down with a friend for a simple cup of coffee, I'm likely to also be checking my phone, shooting off a quick email, and looking around the room to see if there is anyone else I know. And, to be fair, my friend is probably doing the same thing. We accept this breach of loyalty to each other as if it is normal and acceptable, but now I realize this behavior weakens our connection. Going forward, I want to change this.

Cousin Jack Himes and Sean hanging out at the beach on an overcast day.

AN INSPIRATION

I love how Sean was always so loyal to his friends and to every sports team he rooted for. He never gave up on anyone, which is hard to do. I take that as a lesson on how to treat others. He always treated those he cared for with love. Every day I see his picture on the magnet on my refrigerator, and he is a true inspiration to me.

—Cousin Jack Himes

A GOOD FRIEND IS FORGIVING

A friend is a friend is a friend. In Sean's heart, there was no room for a sometimes friend. Sure, he might argue with a friend. He might be hurt by a friend. He might be angry with a friend. But none of that changed the depth or quality of the friendship. That's why his arguments and his hurts were always so short lived. If you were Sean's friend, he couldn't let you feel unhappy.

For instance, like all siblings, Sean and his sisters, Moira and Meghan, fought. Both girls were younger than Sean but were ahead of him intellectually, and this frequently angered Sean. They would argue and argue and sometimes even shout. But then there would be a sudden quiet, and you could count on Sean to break the silence with, "I'm sorry. I apologize." He couldn't hold a grudge, no matter who started the fight, no matter how hurt he felt. His relationship was more important than winning—every time.

He expected the same from others. I remember once having an argument with my wife Dana. As she angrily headed down the hall to the bedroom, Sean couldn't believe I would let her walk off that way.

"You have to say you're sorry," he said. "That was not nice. You need to apologize." He couldn't express the "why" of his command. He couldn't tell me that my relationship should be stronger and more important than whatever it was we disagreed about. But he understood the bottom line: If this person is important to you, you cannot let them feel bad.

For me, forgiveness is often an ego issue. I don't like to be wrong. I don't want to back down. When I feel that I've been criticized, I can hold a grudge. I'm sure Sean felt these things too, but for some reason that I can't explain, he knew how to put aside those negative feelings to rescue a friendship. He was quick to forgive and would always remind the other person, "You're a good friend." I can hear him saying that over and over—to his teammates, to his coaches, to his teachers, to his classmates, to coworkers, and to me. The truth is, *he* was the good friend, and everyone who was lucky enough to be included in his friendship circle knew that he was the glue that kept everyone together.

I want to be that kind of glue among my friends. And I know now that I can't do that unless I learn from Sean's example to make the friendship less about me and more about us.

Live Like Sean

It is clear to me that Sean was the most popular person in both schools he attended and on all his Special Olympics sports teams. Not because he was the best student or athlete—that was not even close—but because he was a good friend to everyone.

When you call yourself someone's friend, does the relationship meet the bar set by Sean? If you would like to have that same kind of popularity built on genuine relationships, follow his example:

- You can't build a good friendship if you're competing with another person. Instead encourage, support, and cheer them on. Push your friends to be the best they can be by focusing on *their* accomplishments, not on your own. Be the confidence booster your friends need, even if it means you lose the game. If you do that, you will be rewarded with good friends who clear the bench to surround you with love and support when you need it.

- Accept your friends for who they are, and expect them to do the same for you. If you really can't stand to listen to so-and-so drone on about their latest life drama, say so, and see if the friendship holds up under this honesty. If you can't accept them as is or if they expect you to fit a certain image, the friendship is not genuine and should be recognized as merely a pleasant acquaintance.

- Stand up for your friends—always. Have their back. Build them up. Praise them when they are not around to hear you. Think about how you talk to others about your friend. Your comments will reveal if you have a genuine friendship with that person or not. Being loyal is an absolute must in a friendship.

- Make sure your friendships are less about you and more about the two of you. If you can do that, you will find yourself being more forgiving and less likely to hold a grudge. Be quick with an "I'm sorry" if that's what it takes to help your friend feel good again. If only one person in the relationship is benefiting, it's not a friendship.

I do not offer this advice like a motivational speaker who has everything figured out. I am still learning. I am still trying. I hope that by following Sean's example, I may someday be half the man he was.

And I hope that his example will help you see through his loving eyes how life can and should be lived.

5

BE LOUD AND PROUD

I am not a quiet man by any means. I enjoy telling a good joke or a funny story with my family and friends around the dinner table. My forebears came from Ireland, and I think the Irish have a special gift of gab. But that gift has the potential to be embarrassing to everyone at my table in a restaurant when people around us start giving me annoyed looks, or worse, a scolding "SSHHH!" Yes, I have been shushed many times in many situations. When that happens, I try to lower my voice, mostly because I don't want my family and friends to feel uncomfortable.

I used to wonder why *they* should feel embarrassed when I'm the one being loud. Then came Sean, and I was on the other side of the table from the one with the booming voice. I, too, was embarrassed.

I was still a new parent when this began to happen. Sean was my first child. I didn't know what to expect or how to control him. When he was little, he could be assertive. He'd shout, "I want to go now!" And he would yell and demand attention. Now I know that all kids do that in public, but at the time I thought my son was the only one, and I would hurry him out of the room so he wouldn't bother anyone. He was embarrassing me.

As he grew, Sean continued to be loud and attract attention. But now his outbursts were rarely a sign of upset; they reflected his joy. Sean had a loud booming voice and could laugh louder than anyone I have ever met. You could count on him to burst out laughing at a joke or scream out in happiness. I had to learn how to love this side of my son and not hide him to cover up my own discomfort.

NO REASON TO APOLOGIZE

It is a memory involving Sean's sister Moira that vividly reminds me to let others be who they are without needing to stop or change them. We were in Chili's in Parsippany (Sean's favorite restaurant) when he was about 18 years old. It was dinner time, and the place was pretty crowded. As we crammed into a booth and our family laughed at some silly joke, Sean burst out with a loud laugh and mumbled words, in typical Sean fashion, that went on for a full minute. That's when I saw 14-year-old Moira giving the death glare to a bunch of high school boys sitting in a nearby booth, making fun of Sean's speech. One of the boys was shamed by her angry face; he immediately got his friends to stop.

It would be understandable if, instead of feeling protective, Moira felt mortified. She might have wanted to crawl under the table to avoid having these guys associate her with her "weird" brother. After all, young teens have an image they want to maintain. But she didn't worry about that. She took care of the situation without a hint of embarrassment, then returned her attention to her family. Moira was one of the first to show me how to love Sean without apology or embarrassment.

Sean was oblivious to his sister's stare-down. It wasn't that he didn't care about other people's feelings; he was very sensitive to everyone else's emotions. But he could never imagine that being happy—laughing and clapping—was something that was bothersome. And because his happiness made us all happy, we learned to simply enjoy it.

That lesson came in handy many times over the course of Sean's life. If we were at a sports bar watching a game and his team hit a home run or scored a touchdown, there was no hiding Sean's enthusiasm; everyone in the place knew who he was rooting for. Of course, some people disapproved of the noise. They gave us nasty looks or made a big show of moving their seats. Should I have apologized to these people? Should I have curbed Sean's enthusiasm? No! I should have suggested that they try—just once—to express the same kind of unrestrained happiness.

By this time, I had learned my lesson. I had learned to enjoy who Sean was: someone who was just being himself. Someone who was loud. Someone who was not embarrassed by his loudness because he had no idea that showing happiness could ever be a bad thing. I would not be embarrassed by that either, and I would certainly not apologize.

CHOOSING LOVE OVER EMBARRASSMENT

Sean with his biggest supporter, his mom, Maggie.

I LOVE YOU TOO

One evening when Sean was about 11 years old, TJ and Maggie were hosting a fundraiser for the Children's Center in Cedar Knolls, New Jersey (now the P.G. Chambers School). Sean was up front near TJ, who was the auctioneer. Maggie was sitting with friends about three seats from the aisle. I was with my friend Warren on the other side of the aisle. All of a sudden, Sean came walking down the aisle toward the back. As he was about to pass us, he looked toward his mother and without breaking stride said in a loud voice, not caring who heard him, "I love you, Mommy." Maggie responded,

"I love you too, Sean." His smile grew larger and his eyes twinkled brighter as he continued down the aisle. Warren and I just looked at each other, feeling the love all around us. It was a beautiful moment.

—Papa Tim

When Sean was 28 years old, I bought a condo in the Water Club at North Palm Beach, Florida. There were two 22-story buildings, and our unit was on the 20th floor overlooking the ocean and the inlet. It was a place for us to get away and spend time together. On his first—and as it turned out, his only—visit, Sean was thrilled that the complex had two pools. One was a lap pool, and the other was a small recreational pool that was about ankle deep where you entered and gradually got deeper until it bottomed out at four-and-a-half feet. On that sunny day in late March, there were about a dozen adults sitting in lounge chairs; my parents were at the tall-top tables at the water's edge. No one was in the pool—until Sean arrived. He threw his 240-pound body into three feet of water with unbounding glee. "This is great!" he yelled for the world to hear. "I love this pool. Do you love this pool, Dad?"

If I hadn't learned to respect the right of my loved ones to express themselves in any way that they wanted, without worrying that their actions reflected on me, this would have been a time for shushing. After all, was this how we wanted to introduce ourselves to our new neighbors—in a loud, messy, exuberant way? Yes, it was! Sean's grandparents and I looked on with proud smiles.

Sean didn't embarrass us, because he was living life to the fullest and enjoying it in a way we all wish we could. Yes, he was spontaneous and loud, but he didn't feel embarrassed at all. I wish I could live more like him every day!

It took a long time for me to get to that place of acceptance, but we learned to feel Sean's joy and take it on as our own without worrying about what others would think.

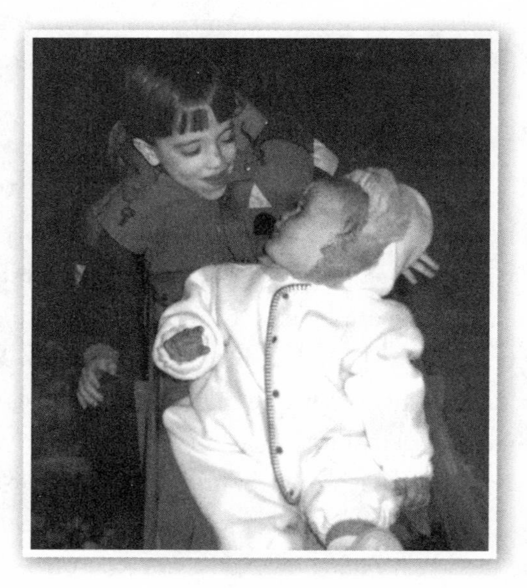

Sean and his cousin Erin Himes have the best seats for a ride in the snow.

A CONTAGIOUS ATTITUDE

What truly impacted me the most deeply was just knowing and loving Sean. His positive attitude was contagious, the way he loved his family was heartwarming, and his honesty was refreshing. Being around him made all of us better, because he was simply himself at all times.

—Cousin Erin Nelligan Himes

BEING LOUD QUIETLY

Sometimes being loud can come through a very quiet action. The celebration of Sean's life after he passed away was held at the Park Avenue Club in Morristown, New Jersey. This large banquet hall is owned by 10 charities—including the Special Olympics—and can accommodate about 800 people. All the tables were filled, and more people were standing all along the back wall. Moira and Meghan had framed pictures of Sean with his friends and put them on every table and all around the room. Sean's mom, his sisters, and I were sitting in the front of the room.

The LETR Honor Guard, which raises tons of money for the Special Olympics, was there along with a bagpiper who played "Amazing Grace" at the beginning. Father Kupke, who had known Sean almost all of his life, led us in some prayers, and then he introduced me.

I gave a eulogy that I knew would rip my heart out, but I held up until the very end, when I gave in to my emotions. I was visibly shaken in front of the hundreds of people gathered in the hall. It was an awkward moment, and I understand why people looked the other way. It's embarrassing to watch a grown man cry. My tears came even harder as a guitar player sang "Beautiful Boy"—John Lennon's tribute to his son, also named Sean. Then something happened that reminded me of how much smarter special-needs people can be than the rest of us.

I didn't see James, Sean's friend and basketball teammate, coming from the farthest corner of the room until he hugged me from behind. "Are you okay, TJ?" he asked, without a hint of discomfort or embarrassment. "I miss Sean so much too," he said. No one else in the room knew how to do that. How to ignore that my tears made them feel uncomfortable. How to let go of their own awkward feelings and focus on mine. That was an amazing moment—a powerful moment. James saw how hurt and vulnerable I was at the end of my comments about Sean's life. James's first instinct—just as Sean's would have been—was to stand up and walk up in front of all these strangers to offer me comfort.

After dinner, my dad got up to talk. (No family event would ever be complete without him grabbing a microphone.) Then he invited anyone present to come up and share a few words about Sean. A few friends of mine stood up and shared memories. And then James again got up and marched to the front of the room. He stood by the mic and in a forceful voice spoke directly to each member of Sean's family and reminded us of Sean's love. He looked out at all the people there and demanded that they follow their dreams. "Sean followed his dreams," he said, "and you have to do that too!" This special young man gave one of the most moving tributes of the day. Loud, unexpected, and unembarrassed.

I FEEL HAPPY IN MY HEART

Sean was my friend. Sean was my teammate on Storm—on basketball. I remember Sean giving Coach Gerie a hug. I always liked Sean's hug or high five. We went to see a hockey game and had fun—a LOT of fun! When I think of Sean, I feel happy in my heart because of his laugh. He was a happy man. Sean made everybody feel like family. I feel sad about Sean because I miss him on my team, and I didn't get to say goodbye. I learned from Sean to be happy. I learned how to follow my heart . . . my dreams. Sean made me feel important, and I miss him a lot.

—James Hackett, a teammate on the Special Olympics basketball team Storm (as told to his mom, Jill)

Live Like Sean

It takes guts to stare down someone who tries to embarrass a loved one for being loud in public.

It takes guts to ignore the *tsks* and shushing when a loved one is being, well, his or her loud self.

It takes guts to put aside your own embarrassment and instead focus on the emotional needs of another.

Yes, it takes guts—the kind that I want to have.

Sean taught me to let him be spontaneous and loud and to not apologize, because his noise came from his heart with an intent that was genuine.

Yes, people with special needs often do get a pass for socially unacceptable behavior. I am not suggesting that loud, spontaneous actions are an ideal we should all strive for. If I routinely ignored the fact that my booming voice was bothering everyone around me in a quiet, candle-lit restaurant, that would be rude. The lesson from Sean is more about acceptance.

So what can we do to absorb that lesson?

- Know who you are.
- Know whom you love.
- And don't worry so much about what others think.

6

BE BRAVE

We all have faced life moments when we needed to be brave. This is most especially true once we have children of our own and our protective instincts click in. We hug our children close and pretend that we're not scared at all as lightning rips the sky open and the thunder cracks above our heads. We sing along to "The Wheels on the Bus" without showing our fear while we wait for help on the side of the highway after a tire blowout. We shoulder on with a confident smile. Most of the time.

But how does your bravery hold up when you're the only one around? When only you know if you have the courage to make a difficult choice? To choose the uncertain path and to move ahead with no guarantee of safety or success? Watching Sean grow, I came to realize that it is these circumstances that test one's true level of courage.

THE PANIC ALARM

I have read that courage can be defined as doing something that frightens you or being strong in the face of pain or grief. If you're not afraid, if it doesn't hurt, there is no need for bravery. By this definition, Sean is my model of bravery because there were so many things that scared him and hurt him, yet he always confronted the fear and came out whole on the other side.

Many of Sean's fears were typical for his age, but they were amplified by his intellectual disabilities. He couldn't always figure out how something was "okay," as his mom and I assured him. He was scared of frightening movies. He pulled back from some new experiences. And when he was little, he hated characters in costumes. I remember being at Chuck E. Cheese for a birthday party when Sean was about five or six. As Chuck E. Cheese started walking toward him, he literally froze. Then he started shaking and screaming, "No! I hate that rat. He's scary!" He was even scared of the costumed Disney characters on our first visit to Disney World when he was seven years old. But in those situations, we could take him away from the thing that scared him. A reassuring hug had incredible power to allay his fears.

Sometimes, however, his mom and I could not simply carry him out of the room, away from the thing that scared him. Sometimes Sean had to face his fears. This was the case every time he had to go to the doctor's office. It's easy to understand where the fear came from—Sean had multiple difficult experiences with doctors, testing, needles, and such—but it was still heartbreaking to see how scared he was each time and so motivating to remember how he fought through the fear.

At two years old, Sean was weak, frail, and skinny. He had so much trouble walking that we thought he might have cerebral palsy. (He did not.) He spent long hours going through painful physical therapy sessions and trying to walk with leg braces that hurt him terribly. At that age, Sean couldn't have found his way to the corner of our street, but if our car turned onto Route 287, he knew we were going to the physical therapist's office, and he would begin kicking and crying, "I don't want to go!" But he always went through with the visit and the exercises.

Being brave in the face of your fears doesn't mean you get over the emotion. Sean had to face his fear of doctors year after year. I remember one incident, when he was about 15, that highlights the depth of his pain and the level of courage it took for him to do the most basic things. It was time for Sean's flu shot, and I was dreading the trip to the doctor's office. (Taking Sean to the doctor was no picnic for me either.) On this day, when I told him where we were going, he ran out of the house and into our pool cabana, yelling, "I'm not going! I'm not going!"

By this time, Sean was five foot seven and weighed around 175 pounds. He was strong. I couldn't just grab him and put him into the car. As we were arguing, he backed up against the wall and set off the pool panic alarm. The noise was ear-splittingly loud, and I knew the police would be coming soon. Now Sean was really scared. He ran down the driveway, along the sidewalk, and into the dead-end cul-de-sac. That's when a police car came zooming down the street with its siren blaring in response to the alarm.

The police officer, Doug Vanderhoof, was a friend of mine. He saw us out on the street and jumped out of this car. "Is everything okay?" he yelled.

"Yep," I said. "This is what happens when we're going to the doctor."

Doug calmed Sean down and convinced him to get into the car, which was a huge help. But I still had to get Sean to the doctor's office.

I can only imagine the amount of courage it took for Sean to put one foot in front of the other and walk himself through the office door where he knew he was going to be hurt. At the time, I was frustrated by the experience. Looking back, I'm in awe.

The Nelligan family gathers in celebration of Sean.

FEARLESSLY AND HONESTLY

I see Sean in all of my cousins, in my aunts, uncles, and grandparents, in every friend of Sean's I've met and interacted with. Each and every person he knew is better because of him. He made those around him feel good, and he inspired me to live a bit more fearlessly and honestly.

—Cousin Erin Nelligan Himes

BEING SCARED FOR OTHERS

Sean had a highly developed sense of empathy that was heartwarming to watch, but it also caused him to suffer when he saw others suffering. That's why he was scared of ambulances. One day when Sean was 18, we were at Yankee Stadium for the All-Star Game with my friend Nick Matarazzo and his son, Mike. As we stood outside the stadium waiting to enter, suddenly we heard a commotion, and we saw someone on the ground getting CPR. Then the police and an ambulance arrived. Sean had a terrible reaction. He started shaking and yelling, "No! No!" He calmed down enough for us to get to our seats, but then he said, "I'm going to throw up!" and ran off to the men's room.

I tried over and over to explain that the ambulance workers were there to help people. But that didn't comfort him until I added that the EMTs usually stop to get the sick person doughnuts. From then on, every time we heard or saw an ambulance, Sean would say, "They're going to get doughnuts, right?" That was his way of coping with a deep-seated fear. It was a literal sugar coating that gave him armor against what some might say was an irrational fear. Irrational or not, his fear of physical therapy, of doctors, and of ambulances was very real.

All of these instances gave me opportunities to watch Sean be brave.

Sean, Dana Nelligan, Grandma Helen, and Papa Tim at the Nelligan Sports Marketing's golf outing to benefit the 2014 Special Olympics USA Games.

SCARED BUT EMPATHETIC

I remember that Sean really did not like going to Morristown Hospital Early Intervention Program. Even at the age of two, he would protest by crying as soon as the car turned onto Route 287. It seemed to me that he had good reason to be worried; although the therapists were probably excellent in the performance of their job, they never made it seem like fun. Lots of the children in the program had many visible medical issues, and Sean was always empathetic to them. Even though he was little and had so many problems of his own, he wanted to find out why the other children had those problems.

—Grandma Helen

SMALL ACTS OF BRAVERY

Sometimes being brave has nothing to do with facing physical pain. It may arise in simple human interactions, as in breaking the awkward silences that follow the delivery of bad news. When a friend loses a job, or gets divorced, or has a death in the family, it takes a bit of courage to get past, "I don't know what to say."

I was reminded of this by my relationship with the NY Giants Assistant General Manager Kevin Abrams. We first met 10 years ago in a restaurant in Hoboken, New Jersey, that was totally empty except for Kevin and his girlfriend, Sean, and me. A snowstorm raged outside. The bartender introduced us, and we started talking about the fact that the Giants were probably not going to re-sign wide receiver Mario Manningham, who had made a spectacular sideline catch for a 38-yard reception in the fourth quarter to help the Giants beat the Patriots in Super Bowl XLVI that year.

Sean listened to the talk about salary caps like we were talking Chinese and then cut to the point: "Kevin, did you see the catch in the Super Bowl or not? Sign him." We all laughed at the direct and simple solution (which the Giants ignored), and the conversation helped pass the time on that cold, snowy night. Then we all went on our way.

I kept in touch with Kevin periodically after that. When I heard in 2017 that the Giants had fired his boss, Jerry Reese, I knew Kevin's own job was in danger. But what do you say to a guy in that situation? It's easier just to keep quiet. When I realized that Sean would never hide behind that excuse, I sent Kevin a quick text, simply saying, "Are you okay?" One second later, he responded, "I appreciate you reaching out. They're going to keep me." And the Giants did. Two years later, when Kevin heard about Sean's passing, he contacted me from London, leaving a voicemail message on my cell phone expressing sympathy. It meant a lot to me.

I think most people don't reach out when bad stuff happens because there's nothing anyone can say to change the terrible event. But I learned from Sean that just being brave enough to initiate a contact, to send a note as simple as "Hello. How are you?" is very meaningful.

FINDING MY OWN COURAGE

At other times being brave has life-changing implications. There wouldn't have been a Nelligan Sports Marketing if there hadn't been a Sean Nelligan. There's no doubt about that. When I was thinking about starting my own company, I was scared at the prospect. I could only imagine the down side: What if I failed? How would I pay my bills? How would my girls go to college? I already had a good job. I was making great money. Why change that?

There was a lot riding on this decision. Then I thought of Sean and all that he had faced and been through.

Why should I be afraid? I asked myself. If Sean could face all the challenges of his life and come out stronger, how could I back away from a challenge? Sean was my inspiration. He gave me the courage to say, "I've been given talents that he doesn't have. He can't do this, but I can. Only fear is holding me back." Because I was afraid, I was overthinking what might happen in the next 20 years, rather than concentrating on what I could do right now.

THE BACK STORY BEHIND NELLIGAN SPORTS MARKETING

In 1990 I was working on Wall Street, and I hated it. Although I was making a lot of money for a guy in his late 20s, I knew I had to get out. So I went to work for Host Communications based in Kentucky. The company had the marketing and media rights to the NCAA basketball championships, including the Final Four, the culmination of the tournament. Host Communications represented many colleges and universities and men's and women's sport teams at places like Notre Dame, Texas, Florida State, and Alabama. I worked for Jim Host, "the godfather of college sports," who had started marketing these athletic programs in the 1970s, before anybody else did.

When I joined the company, it was based in the Southeast; I started the New York office. By 1995 I was president of the Host sports division, running all national sales and selling all the sponsorships to corporate America for the NCAA Basketball Tournament—to 20 of the Fortune 100 companies, including American Express, Nabisco, Hershey, Pepsi, and GM, among others. I worked for Host for nine years and then decided to go out on my own with a noncompete clause.

I started Nelligan Sports Marketing in 1999, representing six schools in the Big East Conference, and a year later ran right into a bad economy. The first thing companies cut in bad times is their advertising budget, since that is a direct savings to the bottom line. But my firm was counting on those advertising budgets. I had hired employees and incurred other expenses. The first year we lost seven-plus figures of income. You bet I was scared. The second year, though, we were finally making money, and over the 15 years that I owned the firm, it took off and became one of the most successful sports-marketing companies in the country.

Nelligan Sports Marketing also gave Sean and his best friend, Bobby, a good job in accounts receivable that they loved. They worked hard, were proud of their work, and were respected by the other employees.

Fear became a temporary stumbling block for me again in 2014, when I thought about selling the company that Sean and I loved. At that time, as the third largest college sports-marketing company in the country, we represented 55 schools and conferences in a multibillion-dollar industry. Learfield Sports, one of the two leaders in the field, made me an incredible offer I couldn't refuse. Though I had trepidations, I went ahead with the deal. In 2018, Learfield and IMG College, the other leader in this area, would merge and become Learfield IMG College, becoming the largest college sports marketing company in the industry.

But the bottom line for the whole adventure was the fact that without Sean as my role model, none of this would ever have happened. Without his example, I would not have had the courage to risk it all.

Live Like Sean

Every day we're called on to be brave. It takes courage to drive a car on an interstate highway at 75 miles an hour, just to keep up with the flow of traffic. It takes courage to walk into work, knowing there will be tasks that challenge our capabilities. It takes a load of courage to believe we can raise children who will be strong, caring, productive members of society.

But there are also life situations that demand the kind of bravery you can accept or turn away from because no one will notice or care. Those are the times when only you know if you have the courage to make the difficult choice. In those moments, try to live like Sean.

- When the big picture is too difficult to handle, just put one foot in front of the other and keep going. Sean walked into the doctor's office with a pounding heart and tearful eyes, one step at a time.

- When you know an important decision may hurt, either physically or emotionally, focus on the benefits that lie on the other side of the pain. Sean learned to cope by focusing on the doughnut rather than the pain.

- When it's easier to be silent, have the courage to get past an awkward moment and offer comfort. Sean would never accept silence when a few words would help soothe someone else's hurt.

- If you've been given talents and abilities that others do not have, don't be afraid to use them. Sean was limited in his abilities. You are not.

- Don't overthink what will happen in the next 20 years if you contemplate a change in your life. Sean didn't get another 20 years, and he didn't get the chance to make major life decisions. Be brave. Make the change. Go for it.

7

BE PROACTIVE

Sean did not have an "I can't do it" attitude, even though he couldn't read, or play video games, or run a race, or ride a bike, or climb a tree, or . . . well, any of the things that most other kids could do. Every day he woke up ready to find the thing that he *could* do. Over time, he found that he could shoot a basketball, play a mean game of bocce, memorize sports team logos, ride a three-wheeled bike, prepare accounts receivable mailings, do restaurant food prep, and on and on.

This attitude—built on the belief that you can shape the direction of your life by actively taking steps to accomplish what you *can* do rather than lamenting what you *can't* do—is a solid definition of the word *proactive.*

As the parent of a special-needs child, I learned the importance of following Sean's example on this. If I expected to maximize his potential, I had to ditch my focus on the things I couldn't do to help him and, with all my heart and drive, go after the things I could do to help my son.

In his early years this was hard, because Sean's doctors, therapists, and counselors were well educated in "can't," and they regularly passed that information on to me and his mom. Fortunately, Sean was not educated like that; he was wired to take his life in his own hands and proactively grab onto everything it gave him. That became my goal, too.

I WILL FIGHT FOR THESE CHILDREN

One of my early opportunities to be proactive like Sean and for Sean came when he was six years old and in first grade. After a thorough evaluation of his intellectual abilities and disabilities, the professionals in the school's Special Services Department created an Individual Education Plan (IEP) as required by the state. This plan outlined Sean's needs in order to progress through the prescribed academic steps. This IEP clearly stated that Sean needed to continue his education through the summer months or else he would regress in his learning. At the end of his first school year, his mom and I found out that the school district would not approve his summer school program or the transportation to get him there. I called the director of special services for the school district to question this decision of denying Sean what his IEP said he needed.

The director told me, "Oh, no, we don't do that. We have never approved summer school for our special-needs children."

"But . . . ," I persisted, "every person on his team says this is what he needs. We have had many meetings with his entire IEP team to come up with his specific IEP," I said. "And they all agree that Sean needs to go to summer school."

"Well," said this very confident voice on the other end of the line, "we don't pay for summer school or the bus for summer school. Never have."

As parents, we fight so many battles for our special-needs kids, it's exhausting. This was an instance when it would have been so much easier to let Sean take the summer off and pick up again in September. But when I thought about the battles he had already fought in his young life and the courage he had to get to this point, how could I not fight for him?

Knowing that a child's IEP is a legal and binding document, I threatened to sue the district. "You are wrong," I reminded the director, "and the law is on Sean's side. I'm coming over."

I immediately drove to his office, and 15 minutes later, as I entered the school building, the director was coming out of his office to meet me.

"It's all taken care of," he said. "Sean can go to summer school, and we'll bus him. But we don't usually do this. This is an exception."

This sudden change of heart didn't exactly make me happy. In fact, it made me angry. I looked the director in the eye and shook my head. "No. You are going to do this for every child whose IEP says you need to do this. I will take on this fight for all of these children."

I knew I was starting what could be a drawn-out, expensive battle, but I just couldn't sit on the couch and accept the "can't" word one more time. Again, I thought of Sean and all the times when he could have taken the easy road and accepted what the experts told him he couldn't do, but he didn't. How could I do less?

Without going to court, the school district agreed to pay for summer school and transportation for all students whose IEPs indicated it was needed. Score one for Sean's team.

CHOOSING A PATH FILLED WITH HOPE AND POTENTIAL

I first decided to become proactive when Sean was four years old, in 1994. An old fraternity brother of mine, Don Slaght, told me about his involvement with Special Olympics New Jersey (SONJ) and invited me to go with him to the Special Olympics Summer Games, which were being held at the College of New Jersey (TCNJ). I had volunteered for Special Olympics in college, but I didn't really know how they might help Sean. Still, I figured what the heck and joined Don with Sean strapped in a backpack.

As we walked around the college fields, I saw crowds of people—families, friends, volunteers, coaches, strangers—all laughing and cheering. I saw athletes of all ages competing with passion and dedication. I couldn't believe it. The scene looked so normal, yet so special. That little trip would forever alter our lives and send Sean, me, and our entire family down a path filled with hope. We would become involved with Special Olympics for the rest of Sean's life, and it would truly change our world.

While I was growing up, sports had been an important part of my identity, so I had spent the last four years grieving over the fact that Sean would not have the challenge of competition or the camaraderie of teammates. Looking around at these athletes, I realized how wrong I had been. Instead of focusing on what Sean could not do, I was starting to feel encouraged by what he possibly could do. He couldn't compete in the town's recreational sports program, but he sure could be an athlete.

The following year, I joined the board of SONJ and remained a member for the next 20 years. At first, Sean was not strong enough to compete in any of the 16 sports offered through the Special Olympics. But when he was 12, things changed. I was chair of the board that year and was giving a welcoming speech as the athletes marched onto the Lion's Stadium field at TCNJ. Grouped by county teams from all over the state, the more than 2,500 athletes came in with proud smiles and high fives, with a bagpiper and an honor guard in front of each delegation. The stands were jam-packed with friends and family, all cheering, whistling, and stamping with encouragement.

Then I spotted him. My boy entered the stadium for the first time as an athlete who could do a 100-yard walk. He walked tall. He walked proud. He was excited and happy, smiling and having a ball. As I watched Sean proceed past the line of hundreds of uniformed law enforcement officers who were giving high fives to each athlete, I knew that this was a watershed moment.

It's hard to describe how I felt. Suddenly my attitude changed from "poor me," filled with anger and focusing on all the things Sean couldn't do, to choosing to live like Sean—walking tall and proud and happy. I wanted to recognize the positives in Sean's life, the talents and strengths he did have, and proactively find ways to maximize those experiences and opportunities. The Special Olympics gave me the perfect venue to do this.

SPECIAL OLYMPICS NEW JERSEY

Special Olympics New Jersey began in 1969 when New Jersey sent six participants to the Eastern Regional Special Olympics Games at the University of Maryland. From that time to the point when I got involved, the organization had done wonderful things for both children and adults with intellectual disabilities in New Jersey. Over the years, 20,000-plus athletes were given the opportunity to compete in different events, local and statewide. The regional events culminated each year with the New Jersey Summer Games at TCNJ, where the athletes stayed in the dorms for the weekend and competed in 14 different sports—from bocce and track to basketball and swimming. The program was wildly successful, thanks to the hard work of thousands of volunteer coaches and family members.

However, the athletes didn't have a home base. They didn't have a place of their own to train and compete. Their families didn't have a central meeting place to gather, learn, and support each other. Why not? Perhaps because too many people said, "You can't do that. It's too expensive. You'll never get it done." But those people didn't have Sean as their role model.

In 2001, while I was chair of the board of SONJ, Nelligan Sports Marketing became intertwined with the organization, and the goal of establishing a home base for our athletes became a reality. But not without obstacles.

Obstacle number one: We needed a place to build. Marc S. Edenzon, who was president of SONJ at the time, had a proactive mindset like my own. He saw that the Prince Tennis Racquet building had abandoned tennis courts on land that we could buy for $4 million. The board approved going forward with pursuing the complex in 2001. Obstacle number two: We needed $4 million. When we launched the fundraising campaign in the fall of that year, the financial market had crashed after the horrific terror attack of 9/11. The firm organizing the campaign and the SONJ board thought we should reevaluate our plan, because the teetering economy was causing widespread skepticism by the community, donors, and corporate leaders. It was another example of a "we can't do this" attitude.

But I figured we had nothing to lose. If we couldn't raise the $4 million, we wouldn't buy the lot and build the facility. But why not try? Marc and I went to work, meeting with companies and individuals to get the needed money. Through our persistence, we found that we were the only ones carrying out a fundraising campaign; other nonprofits were holding back because of the financial uncertainty. Happily, we found great opportunities to secure funding.

In 2002 the Special Olympics New Jersey Sports Complex in Lawrenceville, New Jersey, became a reality. The work to build America's most outstanding facility for our Special Olympics athletes continued over the next five years. The complex grew to become a one-of-a-kind sports campus that gave registered athletes, their families, and the community a place to come together to experience an array of programs and services.

The complex expanded in 2007 with the opening of the Eunice Kennedy Shriver Sports & Training Center—named for the woman who founded the Special Olympics in 1968—which now hosts a variety of conferences, seminars, and meetings. This was followed by the construction of a gym with basketball and volleyball courts and the TD Sports Field, whose regulation soccer field was the first of its kind to be used exclusively for Special Olympics programs. The addition of the Wawa Exercise & Wellness Center gave SONJ athletes an official training center.

Additionally, the Sean Nelligan Foundation raised funds through annual golf outings to build a patio area as a tribute to the athletes, families, volunteers, and sponsors who had contributed to the success of SONJ. The support of the LETR community was also recognized with the Law Enforcement Tribute Walk. Today the patio plays host to Camp Shriver, luncheons, special events, and competitions. To continue its support, Nelligan Sports Marketing also hosted a golf outing for 15 years to benefit SONJ.

With the realization that this magnificent sports complex would become a tangible reminder of a proactive, can-do attitude, I soon set another even bigger goal for our Special Olympics athletes.

A CARING ENVIRONMENT

Sean was charismatic and a giver, and in turn he attracted the attention he so rightly deserved. Sean came by these traits naturally, and they were enhanced by being in an environment that included others who cared deeply for him and others with special needs.

—Aunt Terri Nelligan

USA GAMES

In 2003 I attended the Special Olympics World Games in Ireland. For me, this experience was an inspiration. There were some 7,000 athletes, 3,000 coaches/delegates, and 80,000 families and friends in Croke Park in Dublin with Team USA having the largest delegation of more than 300 athletes. I watched Bono and U2 sing to cheering crowds, and saw Muhammad Ali and many other celebrities march in with athletes from all over the world.

Watching all of this gave me an idea. Why not host an event this big in New Jersey? Marc Edenzon and I had talked about doing something on this scale. We decided to take action. Seven years of planning later, we entered our bid to bring the 2014 USA Games to New Jersey. It would mean hosting the largest and most inspirational national event in the history of Special Olympics, providing an even bigger platform for the athletes to compete and succeed. Our bid beat out Boston—another great accomplishment for our team.

It wasn't long before I became the Chairman and CEO of the

2014 Special Olympics USA Games. In this position, I spent a lot of time assuring all doubters who said, "You can't" (and there were a lot of them!) that I could obtain the $20 million needed for the athletes and their parents and coaches from around the country to be transported to New Jersey, and then compete and stay there during the games, all free of charge.

We planned the campaign using my fundraising expertise and connections and by teaming up with two outstanding can-do guys, Marc Edenzon, who became president of the 2014 Special Olympics USA Games, in addition to holding that post for SONJ, and Tom Varga, who worked for me at Nelligan Sports. I made Tom the Senior VP of Special Olympics USA sponsorship sales. We needed just ten companies to each give us $1 million. And they did. These Founding Partners would become the base of our efforts. We had other levels of support: Gold Medal Sponsor, Silver, Bronze, and so on. At the end of the day we had managed to get more than 62 companies on board and had raised well over $20 million for these games.

We were fortunate to have 21st Century Fox as a Special Olympics Games Founding Partner. The company provided on-air and online media exposure across their cable and broadcast networks, as well as on local stations. Through their affiliate YES network, we were able to film a TV commercial featuring Yankees baseball great Derek Jeter in Yankee Stadium's center field with the Special Olympics logo behind him. This kind of publicity helped encourage others to view our children as we do—as strong, accomplished individuals. It conveyed an important message of acceptance, friendship, and excellence that is developed through participation in athletic competitions by athletes with a wide range of abilities and disabilities.

After all the planning, the opening ceremony was held at the Prudential Center in Newark on June 15, 2014. As the chairman of the Games, I was proud but also humbled to watch the Parade of

Athletes enter the arena. These exceptional people, who all had been told at various times of their lives about all the things they couldn't do, stood before me, every bit as important and valuable in their role in life as any one of us.

If you want to see examples of proactive human beings, go to a Special Olympics event. It will be the most inspirational experience you will ever have. (This is coming from a guy who has been to 25 Final Fours, 10 Super Bowls, two Olympics, and thousands of college sporting events over the years, most often with my passionate sports fan, Sean.)

The next day, the athletes at the USA Games competed to win gold, silver, and bronze medals in 16 different sports competitions: aquatics, athletics, basketball, bocce, bowling, cycling, flag football, golf, gymnastics, powerlifting, softball, soccer, tennis, and volleyball. There were also two new demonstration sports, baseball and a triathlon.

Of course, the athletes couldn't have performed at such a high level nor had such a valuable life experience if they hadn't had the support of 1,000 coaches, 10,000 volunteers, an estimated 70,000 spectators, and more than 15,000 family and friends. And these numbers are just a sampling. Worldwide there are millions of Special Olympics athletes. Yes, it takes a village.

In addition to the competitions, we wanted the athletes to have the time of their lives. To enhance the experience, we brought them to Trenton Thunder baseball games; we arranged four nights of dinner cruises on the Hudson River for a thousand athletes and their coaches each night; and we built an Olympic Village that had a Jersey Shore theme, with sand and boardwalk rides and games.

We also presented a Young Athletes Festival where two- to seven-year-olds were introduced to the Special Olympics program. And finally, we held a Unified Sports Festival in which people from the community participated in sports with Special Olympics athletes.

Sean was one of the 3,500 athletes participating in the 2014 USA Games. He competed in the sport of bocce as part of Team New Jersey. I was proud of him, which had nothing to do with whether or not he would win a medal. (Although I was delighted when he won a gold and a silver medal!) I was most proud of the kind of athlete my son had become. Sean worked hard and long to be the best bocce player he could be, just because. Because he enjoyed the sport. Because he had friends on the team. Because he was part of the team. Because he practiced wholeheartedly to achieve his own personal best. He, along with his fellow athletes, trained for months to demonstrate to the world all that they could accomplish when provided the opportunity. It had been a long road for Sean to get to this moment and one that I will forever cherish.

The fabulous work of the 2014 Special Olympics USA Games Games went on after my involvement that year. The 2018 Special Olympics USA Games held in Seattle, Washington, carried on the torch for these special athletes, and the one planned for 2022 in Florida will, no doubt, do the same. The point of highlighting my role in the 2014 USA Games is to underline my choice to be proactive rather than reactive. By creating opportunities like this for our special-needs children, we allow them to be the best they can be, and we provide an environment of acceptance for who they are as individuals and as equals.

These opportunities are not created by those who retreat in grief, sadness, and disappointment. They happen when the parents and friends of a child with special needs choose a path filled with hope and potential. As a parent of a child with intellectual and developmental disabilities, I know how hard that choice can be. But it would have been even harder for me if I were still sitting on my couch feeling sorry for myself and my son.

Presenting a 2014 Special Olympics USA Games torch to 21st Century Fox executive Kristen Ritter, who tragically died in a car accident in 2015. 21st Century Fox was a founding partner of the 2014 USA Games.

BE PROACTIVE

Special Olympics New Jersey (SONJ) needs to raise approximately $9 million per year in order to operate and provide its athletes with year-round sports programs. In 2018, the Law Enforcement Torch Run in NJ alone raised $4 million, according to SONJ.

Companies interested in finding out more about how they can participate in the movement can visit the organization's website at www.sonj.org.

CHANGE OF FOCUS

For parents who want to maximize the potential of a special-needs child, the challenge is to stop focusing on what they can't do and concentrate on what they can do. Although it may seem daunting at first, if you choose to be proactive, I know there will come a day when you look at your child and you won't see the disability anymore; you will see only their abilities and what they *can* accomplish. You'll also be happily surprised to find that your own grief and anger has diminished and been replaced by acceptance.

This change of focus is not a quick or easy adjustment. I know that from my own experience. But over time, I forgot that Sean couldn't do math and focused instead on his skill in calculating sport scores. I forgot that he couldn't read a book and learned to enjoy the way he could "read" team logos. I forgot that he couldn't ride a two-wheeled bike and was happy to ride next to his adult-size three-wheeler all over town. I forgot that he couldn't play on the town sport teams and signed him up for Special Olympics teams. Once I started seeing all the many things he *could* do, life changed for the better for both of us.

Sean loved working at Nelligan Sports Marketing.

LEARNING LESSONS ABOUT LOVE AND LIFE

My brother and his wife grieved for their son and his future when they were confronted with the realities of Sean's limitations. They were sad. We all were. However, they got up and reset their sights on giving Sean a full and wonderful life. They signed him up for the Special Olympics and supported him in every sport he played; they volunteered at his school for people with special needs; they hosted fundraisers for the school; they brought Sean and his new friends to see concerts; and they spent countless hours watching all of his favorite sports.

When Sean was older, he worked at TJ's company and restaurant, learning more skills and getting along wonderfully with his coworkers, who loved him. Sean accompanied my brother to dinners with his buddies, and eventually Sean felt they were his buddies too. TJ often called Sean "the Mayor," as he was so comfortable with adults, hanging out and talking shop about his favorite teams.

Sean was born into a family of people who never shied away from pushing him to be all that he could be. They never held back at including his friends in family activities, at cheering him on at basketball, bocce ball, and his other Special Olympics triumphs. Sean was included in everything. Loved like crazy. Taken care of. Given the opportunity to thrive. And in return we all learned lessons about love and life.

Sean will be missed by all of us forever. We will strive to

remember to live like him. But I for one will also strive to live like TJ, who redirected his goals as a father, rose above his grief for the son he thought he'd have, and loved the one he did have. Unconditionally. TJ will tell you he loved Sean unconditionally because Sean was so capable of unconditional love himself. And I believe that's true.

—Aunt Eileen Nelligan Corcoran

Live Like Sean

Children like Sean may not appear to have what others consider "normal" God-given abilities, but I have learned that in many ways, they have more abilities—more important abilities—than we have. Living like Sean means cultivating a can-do mindset. Here's how you do that:

- When someone tells you that "you can't," take time to find out if that assessment is undeniably true.
- When someone in a position of power tries to keep your child (or you) down, stand up and fight.
- When you realize you really can't do something (like ride a two-wheeler), look around for what you can do that will give you the same satisfaction. (Ride a three-wheeler!)
- Take one step at a time, no matter how small. Keep walking.

- Set small, realistic goals, and focus on what you *can* do to build your confidence. Then set a new goal to take you further along your life journey.
- Walk tall, proud, and happy.

Having a proactive attitude can be contagious. Watching the way Sean ignored his disabilities and focused with all his heart on the things that he *could* do showed me the power of getting up and making things happen. His actions encouraged me. I hope my actions encourage you. Focus on what *can* be done today.

8

BE ACCEPTING

Anyone meeting Sean for the first time would know that he was "special." His speech, mannerisms, and even his appearance told the world about his struggles. Yet, there were countless times when I would completely forget about his differences because others around us were doing the same. Sean was accepted in all my business and social activities as my son. Just that. Not "the special-needs" son, not the "intellectually challenged" son. Just my son. He went with me everywhere because today's society has become more accepting of people with intellectual and developmental challenges. If anyone felt uncomfortable around Sean, that was their problem—not Sean's nor mine. He was right next to me at business functions, social events, fundraisers, and ball games—everywhere I went.

He was also accepted where he worked at Nelligan Sports Marketing and at the Montville Inn. Was this because I was the boss and the other employees had no choice? I don't think so. The clients and customers who interacted with Sean and his friend and coworker Bobby seemed to be genuinely accepting of the pair. They talked and laughed with them. "Did you see that catch by the outfielder in last night's game?" the boys asked. They shared the details of their day and lives: "How is your granddaughter feeling, Mrs. Phibbs?" They complimented each other on their accomplishments: "You did a good job cleaning up that table!" Sean told Bobby or vice versa. Sean grew up and worked in the company of wonderful people who reacted to him as they would react to any other person in their lives.

When Sean was little, I worried a lot about how the world would treat him. As he came of school age, I dreaded the possibility that he might be bullied, ridiculed, or shamed in his time away from his family. Fortunately, he always went to schools that specialized in educating children with special needs, and he spent his days surrounded by caring, supportive teachers and people, so I don't believe he was ever hurt in that way. But I know this is not the case for all children with intellectual and developmental disabilities. His best friend, Bobby, who was mainstreamed in public schools, told me often of his struggles with kids who would knock the books out of his hands, try to trip him, call him names, and so on.

As Sean grew older and spent more time out in the world, sometimes he would get himself into trouble because people wouldn't know that his "inappropriate" behavior was due to his disabilities. One time, for example, we were at a local restaurant, and Sean started staring at a man at the bar. That was just something he did sometimes. But the guy noticed and yelled at him, as if looking for a fight, "What the hell is wrong with you?"

I went over and explained that Sean was my Special Olympics athlete (my way of explaining his disabilities) and meant no harm or insult. After I intervened, people always backed off with an apologetic smile and perhaps a kind word, accepting that the objectionable behavior was, in fact, merely a sign of interest or curiosity.

THE DISGRACE OF "INSANE ASYLUMS"

Unfortunately, the path to the acceptance of special-needs people has been a long and often sad one in the United States. Entire books have been written about the inhumane treatment given to the mentally ill in insane asylums. In my own quick research on the subject, I was reminded of the power of words to shame and hurt. In the past, a boy like my loving, gentle, happy Sean would have been called a retarded, feebleminded, dull, problem child. These words were not thrown around by ignorant people but by the very doctors who "treated" mental illness. In fact, the *Columbia Electronic Encyclopedia* notes that levels of IQ were once identified by the terms of "moron" (IQ of 51–70), "imbecile" (26–50), and "idiot" (0–25).

Until the mid-1900s, children like Sean would likely have been institutionalized and hidden away from society. Then, in 1963, President John F. Kennedy signed the Community Mental Health Act, authorizing federal grants for community-based mental healthcare centers offering treatment, diagnosis, and delivery of mental health prevention services. This shifted resources away from institutionalized care to community and home care.

But the horrid conditions in many American insane asylums continued. One of the worst examples was found in the Willowbrook State School in Staten Island, New York. From 1947 to 1987, it was the largest state-run institution in the United States for children with intellectual disabilities. The school was built to hold 4,000 patients, but when Senator Robert Kennedy toured the facility in 1965, it housed 6,000. In a report of his visit, published in part in *The New York Times*, Kennedy found that the residents of this school were "living in filth and dirt, their clothing in rags, in rooms less comfortable and cheerful than the cages in which we put animals in a zoo."

Claims of physical and sexual abuse and even medical experimentation followed. What a heartbreaking thought.

Finally, in 1972, WABC-TV investigative reporter Geraldo Rivera won a Peabody Award for the exposé *Willowbrook: The Last Great Disgrace*. This brought national attention to the treatment of people with intellectual disabilities and pushed the passage of a federal law: The Civil Rights of Institutionalized Persons Act of 1980. With the development of medications to stabilize many mental health conditions and the introduction of Medicaid to pay for at-home and community care, more laws were enacted in every state to limit involuntary hospitalization, so people couldn't be committed without their consent, unless there was a danger of hurting themselves or others.

The change has been astounding. According to a PBS *Frontline* report, in 1955 there were 558,239 mentally ill patients in the nation's public psychiatric hospitals. By 1994 that number was reduced by approximately 92 percent. Certainly, there have been unintended problematic consequences of deinstitutionalization. Many people who would benefit from institutional supervision have been released to fend for themselves; some say this is a major cause of the increase in the homeless population. This, of course, is unfortunate and points to areas of mental health care that still need to be addressed by legislators. But for children like my son, the changes in public attitude and in government support have been a blessing.

COMMUNITY ACCEPTANCE AND INCLUSION ON THE RISE

We are not at the finish line yet. Freeing individuals with disabilities to live and grow in their local communities does not give them automatic acceptance into that community. That is the work of inclusion that must continue. Watching Sean work, play, and compete side by side with people from our family, community, and workplaces gave me back the pride and hope I had lost when I received the devastating news that my son was not "normal." I slowly learned that there was a place for him in the world—a valuable, meaningful, and important place.

I want all families of special-needs individuals to learn from the example of Sean's loving and welcoming view of all people. I want them to learn, as I did, that their loved ones can be welcomed and accepted into the communities where they live. Even today, however, that acceptance is only slowly evolving. But by becoming active in outreach organizations that strive tirelessly to create opportunities for people with and without disabilities to work together, the goal of social acceptance grows closer to a reality every day.

A few organizations that can help families reach this goal include the Special Olympics Unified Sports, Best Buddies, and Special Olympics R-Word Campaign.

Unified Sports: As I discussed in detail in Chapter 7, Special Olympics strives to empower individuals with intellectual disabilities through sports participation. Aiming for even greater social inclusion through shared sports training and competition experiences, the Special Olympics Unified Sports program joins people with and without intellectual disabilities on the same team. The program—started by Robert "Beau" Doherty, president of Special Olympics Connecticut—was inspired by a simple principle stated on its website: "Training together and playing together is a quick path to friendship and understanding."

UNIFIED SPORTS

About 1.4 million people worldwide take part in the Special Olympics Unified Sports program, breaking down stereotypes about people with intellectual disabilities. If you would like more information about Unified Sports, visit its website at www.playunified.org.

After attending the Special Olympics USA games in 2014, my niece Molly and nephews Mac and Connor Strange-Boston began working to get their high school in Virginia to create a Unified Sports team. To say it took persistence is an understatement. Some members of the administration were not keen on the idea. It was just too much work, they said. Mac was not deterred. He recruited one of his best friends, and they tackled it together. A year and a half later, they held the first track meet. The team is still in full force. The younger siblings Connor and Molly run it now, and the whole school enjoys either being a part of it or being fans at the meets. This is the kind of influence Sean had on his cousins.

In 2008 the U.S. Office of Special Education Programs at the U.S. Department of Education joined with Special Olympics to promote greater tolerance of special-needs students and funded Special Olympics Unified Champion Schools. Today Unified Sports programs are in more than 4,500 elementary, middle, and high schools in the United States. This is the kind of progress that gives me hope for a future world where people like Sean will live side by side with their peers in all activities of daily living. I believe that the inclusive attitude that begins on the sports field will extend to the classroom, the workplace, and the community.

Best Buddies: This organization, active in all 50 states and in 54 countries, is described on its website as "the world's largest organization dedicated to ending the social, physical and economic isolation of the 200 million people with intellectual and developmental disabilities (IDD). Our programs empower the special abilities of people with IDD by helping them form meaningful friendships with their peers, secure successful jobs, live independently, improve public speaking, self-advocacy and communication skills, and feel valued by society."

BEST BUDDIES

Best Buddies International is a nonprofit 501(c)(3) organization dedicated to establishing a global volunteer movement that creates opportunities for one-to-one friendships, integrated employment, leadership development, and inclusive living for individuals with intellectual and development disabilities (IDD). For more information, visit its website at www.bestbuddies.org.

In this description, I especially like the phrase "empower the special abilities of people with IDD." I've seen these special abilities in action in Sean, in his classmates, and in his fellow teammates. They all had special abilities that so-called normal people can only wish for. Every chapter of this book is a testament to those abilities and why we must continue to make sure that our special-needs loved ones feel valued by society.

Cousins Shannon and Erin Himes give Sean a Best Buddies t-shirt.

BECAUSE OF SEAN

Sean changed my life in more ways than I could have imagined or even realized as they happened. When I started high school, I joined Best Buddies, eager to connect with my classmates with disabilities. Because of Sean, I knew that, disability or not, we all have more in common than it may initially appear. And, of course, we did—many of the friendships I made in Best Buddies are lifelong.

—Cousin Erin Nelligan Himes

I am proud that my nieces Erin and Shannon and nephew Jack Himes are three of those people, inspired by Sean, who have worked with Best Buddies to help their peers reach this goal.

Special Olympics R-Word Campaign: "What a retard!" I hear this phrase far too often from otherwise smart, caring people who are "just kidding" as they heckle a friend who makes a mistake on the golf course, trips on a curb, or spills a drink on the counter. They mean no harm, but these words *are* harmful—and hurtful. The term "mental retardation" is a medical term for a disorder characterized by a low IQ. The word "retard" is simply a mean, derogatory word that insults all individuals with mental retardation. To distance itself from the hurtful term, the medical condition itself is now more often referred to as "intellectual disability."

SPREAD THE WORD TO END THE WORD

The Special Olympics campaign to end the "R" word is catching on. At the time of this writing, in 6,000-plus schools in 80-plus countries, more than 800,000 people have signed the pledge and made a commitment to take a specific action to eliminate the words "retard" and "retarded" from popular use.

To make a pledge or to bring this campaign to your school, visit the website at www.r-word.org.

To educate the general public about the hurtful impact of calling someone a "retard" and to eliminate the word from our popular vocabulary, the Special Olympics has created a program called "Spread the Word to End the Word." During its annual National Awareness Day, people worldwide are encouraged to pledge to stop using the words "retard" and "retarded."

It's time to stop the "R" word from hurting special-needs people. When someone kiddingly mocks a friend by calling that person a "retard," all people with intellectual disabilities are insulted. That's not okay, and I, for one, pledge to stand up and speak up.

IT'S NOT THE OUTER PACKAGING—IT'S WHAT'S INSIDE

Before Sean, I would not have been comfortable talking with or even making eye contact with someone drooling in a wheelchair with arms flailing in muscle spasms. But then I watched how Sean interacted with ease with every human being he encountered. He was accepting of everyone around him—everyone. He would never base his reaction to people on the way they looked, the clothes they wore, the color of their hair or their skin, the number of their tattoos, or the size of their body. He judged people on who they were on the inside. Even among people with disabilities so much more severe than his own—people in wheelchairs, people who couldn't talk, people who couldn't control their body movements—he never hesitated to offer a warm greeting. Sean knew this was just a human being like himself, just packaged differently.

Now, as if Sean is holding my hand and leading me forward, I can easily approach any special-needs person with a simple, "It's awesome to see you, buddy. How are you today?" And if it turns out that the person doesn't understand me or can't respond to me, nothing is lost. There's no harm done. In fact, the person accompanying the disabled person usually is touched that another human being has gone out of his way to simply say hello. We can all do better at accepting people with all degrees of disabilities for who they are as valuable human beings.

There were times when Sean would strike up a conversation with someone he really should not have. Once in New York City, for example, as we were walking down the street by the convention center, Sean yelled out a hello to a very large, disheveled, angry-looking man who shouted back, "What did you say to me? What did you say?" Then he began approaching us aggressively. Oops. Time to grab Sean's hand and head the other way. But there was no way Sean would do anything differently the next time he saw a person with that kind of appearance or any kind of appearance. He was not afraid of people, because he never looked at the outer packaging. He looked for what was inside each person. Were they kind? Nice? Funny? Did they return his smile or his hello? Those were his criteria of judgment.

Live Like Sean

It is likely that you, as the reader of this book already have a warm spot in your heart for special-needs children and that you have already accepted these beautiful kids for who they are. As our society learns to accept and respect those with disabilities as people with feelings, talents, ambitions, it's my challenge to you to live like Sean, to accept all people—with or without disabilities—with charitable judgment.

Everybody has hardship in their lives. We don't know their stories. Maybe the waitress who messed up my order has an eviction notice waiting for her at home. Maybe the guy who cut me off in traffic has a sick child in the back seat who needs immediate medical attention. Maybe the store cashier who seems rude and curt has been working on her feet for the last 10 hours. Maybe . . .

Maybe . . . Maybe . . . Why can't I extend kindness to each one without knowing their special circumstance, as I expected others to offer kindness to Sean?

And what about incorporating acceptance into our daily relationships with family, friends, and colleagues? What kind of superficial judgments do we make without considering what's really important?

Certainly I've made negative comments in the past about people covered in tattoos and body piercings. I didn't understand why anyone would do that to themselves, and so I was judgmental. Then I watched Sean make friends with people different from himself without thinking twice about how they looked, how they dressed, or even what they believed. And I've tried to put my prejudices aside.

Living like Sean means asking ourselves some basic questions:

- Can I be more accepting of people who look different from me?
- Can I be more accepting of people with political opinions that differ from my own?
- Can I be more accepting of those who have different religious beliefs?
- Can I be more accepting of those who have a nontraditional sexual identity? And on and on.

Thinking about how Sean would react to any of these differences puts these questions in perspective. If the person had a kind heart, he accepted them. Period. Living like Sean reminds me that, in the end, that is all that matters.

Sean with Mom, Maggie, and maternal grandfather, Edward "Ned" McMorrow, and TJ at his baptism.

Sean's first birthday.

Sean in the lead as he climbs higher and higher.

Sean, age 5, at home in Montville, NJ.

TJ and Sean with their favorite storybook.

Moira, cousin Erin Himes, and Sean dancing at Aunt Terri's wedding.

Sean with his sister Moira.

Sean with his sisters and mom.

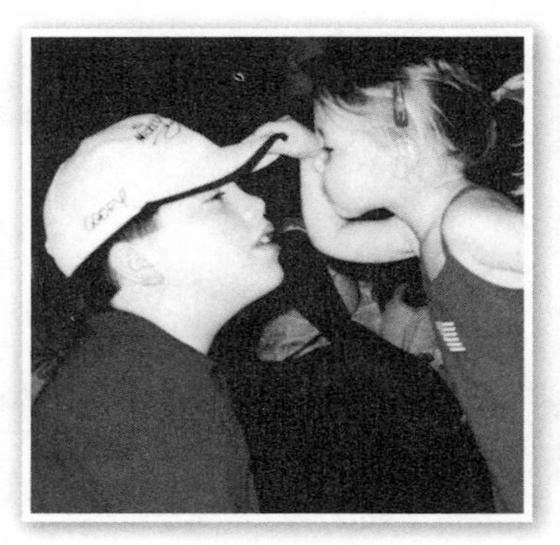

Acceptance begins with his sister Meghan.

Sean with his mom, Maggie, and their dog, Charlie.

Sean showing his love for his sister Meghan.

Sean with his sister Moira, who let Sean be loud and challenged anyone who didn't like it.

Sean and TJ at the opening of the gym at the Special Olympics New Jersey Sports Complex.

Meghan and Sean spending quality time together.

Sean, Dana Nelligan, and TJ at home in Hoboken.

Sean and TJ in Hoboken for Christmas Eve.

Sean celebrates his birthday with his friend, teammate, and colleague, Bobby Fredericks, at the Montville Inn.

Sean with TJ in the NJ Governor's Office for the 2014 Special Olympics USA Games announcement.

With his mom, Maggie, like there is no one else in the world around.

Sean meeting up with Hoboken neighbor Eli Manning.

Sean's Special Olympics medals displayed at his memorial.

Sean and TJ at a New Jersey Devils hockey game.

Sean with his neighbor and friend Buddy "The Cake Boss" Valastro in Hoboken.

Impressing Stephanie McMahon of the WWE during a 2014 Special Olympics USA Games promotional event.

9

BE HAPPY

What does *happy* feel like? When trying to answer that question, many of us can bring up the memory of a moment of pure joy, when our stomach ached from laughing so hard. For me, the moment that comes to mind was in 2013, when Sean and I were washing my car in the driveway of our beach house. After we soaped up the car, Sean was starting to rinse off the suds when suddenly he turned the hose on me. I didn't think it was funny at all, and I yelled at him to stop. As I ran to get away from him, he started chasing me around the car, laughing uncontrollably as I got wetter and wetter. Who could resist that laugh? Soon, I admitted defeat and started laughing too. That was a perfect moment of happiness—spontaneous, simple, and authentic. Finally, Sean dropped the hose, gave me a big hug, and said, "I'm sorry, but that was fun. I love you, Dad." Just thinking about that three-minute moment makes me happy even today.

That kind of laugh-out-loud happiness was a big part of Sean's life. He was always ready to enjoy the moment. But this is not the only kind of happiness that I learned from him. For Sean, happiness was also a daily attitude. He woke up saying, "Good morning! It's going to be a great day." And almost always it was. When the day begins with this kind of attitude, happiness is likely to follow.

Yet, for most of the world's population, happiness is hard to find.

THE PURSUIT OF HAPPINESS

The U.S. Declaration of Independence tells us that the "pursuit of happiness," along with life and liberty, is an unalienable right given by our creator to all humans. You'll notice, however, that our founding fathers did not say that we have a right to happiness—merely that we have the right to pursue it. The actual attainment of happiness is much more difficult, maybe because we're not exactly sure what happiness is.

Is happiness a goal to strive for? Is it a feeling of joy that comes and goes? Is it an innate characteristic that some people have and others don't? Is it within our power to attain, or is it controlled by our circumstances? Apparently, no one really knows.

Despite the fact that happiness is a rather vague state of being, I was amazed to read in *Psychology Today* that researchers find that "people from every corner of the world rate happiness more important than other desirable personal outcomes, such as obtaining wealth, acquiring material goods, and getting into heaven." Wow! Although this is an amazing statement, I find it completely believable, considering that an Internet search of "happiness" brings up 946 million Google hits and that Amazon stocks 40,000 books on the subject. There are a lot of people looking for happiness, including philosophers, theologians, and psychologists who have long tried to identify and package the path to happiness without much success.

So for me to write a chapter called "Be Happy" might seem a bit arrogant. But I have had the advantage of living with the one human being I have ever known who truly did possess the secret to happiness. Certainly Sean's life also held times of sadness, hurt, and anger, but the dominant emotion that drove his short life forward each day was genuine happiness.

Sean didn't need a therapist, medication, or a guidebook to be happy. He just was. I'm not suggesting that we can all acquire his inherent joyfulness as our dominant daily attitude; we have worries and concerns of adulthood that Sean did not have to deal with. And I'm not expecting that this chapter will give you the coveted key to lifelong happiness. But after thinking long and hard about Sean's attitude, I can tell you why it is so hard for many high-functioning people to find their own slice of happiness: They're looking in the wrong places.

Sean encouraged everyone to make signs for the Taylor Swift concert, knowing it would make everyone laugh and have more fun.

STOP LOOKING AT EVERYBODY ELSE

GET LUCKY

When I was visiting Long Beach Island (LBI) in 2013, Sean and I went out to run some errands. We had the top down in the Jeep as we cruised LBI doing something that I cannot remember six years later. What I do remember is Sean dancing and singing in the back seat to his favorite song, "Get Lucky."

Sean wasn't putting on a show for my benefit. His song came on the radio, and he was enjoying the moment for all it was worth. I did not know until that moment how much Sean loved music. Now, I will never forget it.

—Uncle Mike Nelligan

When I first got my job on Wall Street, I was young and ambitious. I wanted to be the best, which meant that I needed to be better, do more, and climb higher than my colleagues. Later when I first got into sports marketing, I was still on that quest to outsell the other guy. I was sure that when I got to the top, I would finally be happy.

People like me, with type-A personalities, have a competitive nature that comes with our high expectations. We expect to work hard and be rewarded for that work. We expect to achieve lofty goals. We expect life to work out the way we plan. None of these expectations are bad or wrong, but life often slaps us back down to reality, which causes our emotions to take a dive. Watching Sean happily live the life that God gave him made me realize that my competitive life was not bringing me what I was after.

Imagine if Sean based his happiness on how his accomplishments compared to others. Since he couldn't read, write, or drive a car, he would see himself as an unhappy loser. But his happiness did not depend on any comparisons. In fact, his level of happiness increased as the success of those around him increased. When we watched my friend's son, Mike Matarazzo, pitch for the Montclair State University baseball team, Sean never voiced any disappointment that he couldn't play on that level too. He was genuinely happy when Mike threw a strike and cheered on his every effort. He was excited and enthusiastic at every game. When his sisters graduated from high school, Sean was the happiest person at the commencement ceremonies. When we went to Syracuse University to visit Sean's younger sister, Meghan, Sean said to me, "Meghan is so lucky to go to Syracuse!" For a moment, I wondered if he was feeling gypped that he didn't get to go to college, but seeing the look on his face, I knew that he was just feeling happy for his sister.

The secret of happiness is often lost today, when social media has made comparison a major league sport with thousands of scorekeepers. Someone might post a vacation picture, for example, and feel happy about the trip, but when the post gets only 25 likes compared to a friend's vacation photo with 1,532 likes, suddenly the joy surrounding the entire vacation is ruined. Judging the value of one's life by poring over social media only feeds our craving for acceptance. In the end, too often social media just makes people miserable, even though we know that the beautiful mansions we see pictured are often filled with very unhappy people.

I gave up my Facebook account when I began to feel that my posts were no more than public bragging. Instead I admired the way

Sean used his Facebook page (with my help); although I would sometimes post a picture on Sean's Facebook page of him at a special event, he never thought about doing that. His Facebook friends were his relatives, his sisters, cousins, aunts, and uncles—and his Special Olympics teammates. He liked to see the pictures on their posts and enjoyed finding out all the good things that were going on in their lives; this brought him happiness. He used his Facebook page to praise his teammates and say "happy birthday" to family and friends. He just enjoyed sharing in the good times of the people he loved.

Sean's brand of happiness, which is not rooted in competition, requires a degree of humility. Sean couldn't define the word "humility," but he had it. He never boasted or bragged. After winning a gold medal at the Special Olympics, for example, he would be happy, but that was the end of it. He never told his classmates the next day what he had done. He never once put down someone who didn't get a medal or who got a bronze medal instead of a gold.

After he went to a Taylor Swift concert, or on vacation to St. Thomas, or even to a big sports event like the Super Bowl, he never would show off to anyone or tell his friends and classmates, "Listen to what great things I did." If someone asked him about an event, he would be delighted to share every detail. Talking and sharing experiences was something he loved to do. But it was always with the goal of sharing his happiness, not of bragging.

Bobby Fredericks, TJ, and Sean on the last day of the Montville Inn.

A PRANKSTER

Doing anything with Sean was fun, because it was nearly impossible to have a bad day when you were with him. One day when we were working at the Montville Inn, I noticed that the buckets of new fries didn't have any water in them yet, so I asked Sean why he didn't fill them with water. The next thing I know, Sean was taking the bucket of water meant for the french fries and dumping it over my head. This was just one of the many times that Sean pranked me. While I was extremely unhappy at first, I think that it was Sean's way of telling me to "lighten up."

—Best friend and coworker Bobby Fredericks

Even in sports, where competition is the basis of the game, Sean never needed to beat out everyone else in order to be happy. Sure, like any athlete, Sean was happy when his team won a soccer or basketball game. But when his team lost, he'd just shake his head and say, "We'll get 'em next time, but I had fun." His reason for being involved in the sport wasn't to get the win or to impress his family and friends; it was to be with his teammates and to enjoy the sport. This is not a philosophy that higher-level, elite sports can thrive on, but for most of us who compete each day in the minor leagues of life, this attitude of friendship and fun over competing and winning is a sure road to more happiness.

STOP LOOKING FOR HAPPINESS IN THE FUTURE

It took me years of climbing the competitive ladder of success to learn that happiness is *not* a destination to be reached in the future. A life that's built on the expectation of future rewards makes it difficult to enjoy the journey, because the end is never reached. Every goal that is met is replaced with another higher, more challenging, more competitive goal. The ultimate goal is always somewhere in the future.

Many people make this same mistake in their search for happiness. *When I get a promotion, I'll be happy. When I have more money, I'll be happy. When I get married, I'll be happy*. Maybe. But this attitude assumes that there is no happiness to be had along the way, and that is something Sean would never understand.

Sean always found something to be happy about, right now. While he planted seeds each day that would grow into accomplishments that would bring him happiness in the future—like learning to walk or play basketball—he never talked about the future. He found his happiness in every experience and every person he was involved with at the moment.

I can see exactly where the switch was flipped in my own life. During my first 10 years in sports marketing, I was so focused on getting from point A to point B that I didn't slow down to appreciate what I was doing and experiencing. I have no pictures of the awards, events, or people I worked with. I couldn't slow down long enough to preserve a memory. My recollections of those years blur together in a rush of activity. Then, when I started Nelligan Sports Marketing and Sean was very often at my side, I learned from him to take time to enjoy the journey. I couldn't help but stop to snap a picture to capture his joy, his big smile, his happy moment. I still had high expectations for the company, but now I was stopping to enjoy what I was doing, and I found myself much happier in the process. Those pictures remind me of the happiness that exists every day in our lives, just waiting to be recognized.

Sean always showing off that smile.

FINDING JOY

There are not many people that you come across in your life who exude pure joy, but Sean was one of them. He loved his family and friends fiercely and without expectation. Sean could brighten anyone's day without even trying, just by being unapologetically himself. There are people who come into your life for a purpose. I believe Sean was put in our lives, if only for a short time, to remind us to find joy. To find joy in both the ordinary and spectacular parts of life and to remember that if we look for it, we can find joy in anything.

—Cousin Kelly Bryant

STOP LOOKING FOR HAPPINESS IN MATERIAL THINGS

Back in the '80s when the Michael Douglas movie *Wall Street* came out, "Greed is Good" became a popular slogan. At that time there was also a bumper sticker that said, "He who dies with the most toys wins." Those sayings have stuck with me all these years, and, I admit, were part of my own life philosophy when I was younger. The idea plays into the belief that we should work to get more money so that we can get more happiness. But Sean was very happy and he had no money, so what does that mean?

At this point, you might be saying to yourself, "Sure, it was easy for Sean to be happy without money, because his parents were wealthy and all his needs were met." I'm not going to argue that money can't buy things that bring happiness: the best medical care, vacations, concert and sports tickets, and so much more. I am blessed that I was able to give these things to Sean. But I know in my heart that these were not the reasons for his happiness. Sean did not know the difference between a $10 bill and a $100 bill. I would often kid him and say, "You got your credit card? This is going to be expensive." "Stop!" he'd say. "You know I don't have money. You're teasing me." I am absolutely sure that if we lived in a one-room apartment and never went on vacations, and never saw concerts or professional sporting events, he'd still be happy. Material things just didn't matter to him.

Sean didn't want six sports jerseys or ten pairs of sneakers, or the latest cell phone, or video games, or a big-screen TV. When someone would offer to buy him a sports cap at an athletic event, Sean would say, "I already have a hat." He was happy with what he had and never wanted more things. That's not where he found his happiness.

For the rest of us, it's hard not to expect more things to bring more happiness. The world of advertising is firmly rooted in making us feel like we don't have enough. After all, if we were happy with what we had, why would we buy more? The trick is to ignore the din of "buy this, buy that" and learn to look for happiness in other places.

Sean feeling happy with cousin Ryan Nelligan.

MY ROLE MODEL

Sean had a contagious smile and always seemed genuinely happy to talk with me. I admired his ability to make everyone he interacted with feel like they were special. Sean was a great role model; I strive to be more like him every day.

—Cousin Ryan Nelligan

STOP LOOKING FOR WAYS THAT OTHERS CAN GIVE HAPPINESS TO YOU

We so often think of happiness as a state of being. "I want to *be* happy," we say. And then we wonder how to make that happen. From watching Sean, I came to realize that happiness isn't showered on us by the universe simply because we wake up in the morning. Very often, it's given in return for our efforts to reach out to others and share a piece of ourselves.

Sean would do this in many ways. I know he felt especially happy when he was being useful and productive. When Sean would sweep the porch and clean the tables at the Montville Inn, the other employees and our customers would often comment on how helpful he was, and he would beam with happiness. When he helped me at Nelligan Sports by stuffing envelopes, he was very happy because he was contributing to our business. Over and over again I saw how his desire to help others opened the door for happiness to enter.

In our own careers, we work hard and we set goals, but too often the actual work does not make us happy. Perhaps we're thinking too hard about what we are getting out of the work, how we can climb higher, how we can get acknowledgment for our efforts, or how we can make more money, rather than thinking about what our work is doing for others. The questions we ask ourselves should be: How can my job be productive and useful? How can I help those I work with? How can I contribute to the company?

You're probably seeing a pattern here: Sean's happiness came from reaching out to others to share his happiness, rather than from getting and taking and having for himself. Being happy was not about more money, more power, more things. It was about his relationships with other people.

This ingredient of Sean's happiness was rooted, I think, in

self-confidence. Sean entered a room without hesitation. He didn't wait to see who would approach him. He immediately walked up to people to say, "Hello, how are you?" And then to express his interest in each person. He didn't worry "Will they like me?" "Should I act a certain way?" All the social insecurities that keep many people from feeling happy did not affect Sean in the least. His happiness came from giving to others of himself—his time, his attention, his hugs, his smiles, his love.

The great thing about this kind of happiness—the kind that comes from sharing rather than taking—is that it is contagious. Sean put everyone else at ease, and from there they simply had to fall into his good mood. Hugs, smiles, and compliments go a long way to spreading the joy. When Sean entered with his big smile and happy demeanor, suddenly the mood of a whole room would be lighter. This even rubbed off on strangers. For example, when we would stop for gas and Sean headed to the convenience store for a snack, he would always hold the door open for others, whether it was two people or ten, and say to each person, "Hi! How are you today?" I could see that almost everyone liked that brief encounter. They would smile back, and just for a moment, they seemed happier than they were before they met Sean.

Imagine if we all could do this. I am now constantly aware of how this happy attitude changes everything—even just a trip to the bank or the store. I can easily make the effort to hold the door and smile. To say hello to people. To simply be friendly. It's really not that hard.

Live Like Sean

As I write this chapter, the holidays are near. It's my first Thanksgiving, Christmas, and New Year without Sean. You can understand why I'm not feeling happy. But, if I didn't feel this pain and go through this difficult time, I wouldn't see the beauty in Sean's life and recognize how it has affected me and has the continuing ability to make me a better—and happier—person. Part of me died with Sean, but I also now see that part of him lives on in me forever.

For Sean—and for all of us—being happy comes down to certain precepts we can all adopt in our daily life:

- Don't compare. To live like Sean, be happy for other people without jealousy or comparisons. Although many business pursuits require us to advertise our accomplishments and broadcast our successes, this is rarely true in our personal lives. Try on some humility and see if being free of the burden of self-promotion doesn't make you feel happier. Then cut down on your social-media scrolling time. Psychologists are finding that following the posts of our friends often makes us feel like we're missing out. We begin to believe that others are more successful than we are and that they definitely are happier. All of this makes us unhappy, so why do this to ourselves? Unplug occasionally to reduce the temptation of comparison.

- Be happy now. When you get out of bed tomorrow, you have a decision to make. Am I going to be happy? You choose. Do not wait for your happiness to come about through some accomplishment in the future. Bring it into your life each day. Remind yourself that the mind cannot hold a happy thought and a negative thought at the same time, so choose the happy thought. Don't argue with your colleague over who jammed the copy machine. Don't lash out at the aggressive driver. Don't snap at the waitress who messes up your order. Don't bite back at someone who insults you. Choose to live happy one day at a time.

- Take the price tag off happiness. More clothes, more electronics, more housewares, or more toys won't make you happy. Instead, focus your search on the people in your life. Relationships were the place where happiness was anchored in Sean's world. He was happiest when he was with those he loved—family, friends, colleagues, teammates—and when he could give something of himself to those people.
- Instead of looking for ways to *get* happiness, start looking for ways you can *give* happiness to others. Start simple: Open a door, say hello, give a compliment. Work on building relationships that can help you uncover the joy in the simple things, like talking, eating, and laughing. Your moment of bliss may not be like mine and involve a garden hose, but if you keep your heart open to the possibility of finding happiness in your daily interactions with other people, happiness will find a way inside.

Once you make the effort to bring happiness into your world, into your relationships, and into your heart, you will begin to know what it is like to live like Sean. You too will jump up to dance when you hear Pharrell Williams sing "Happy." Sean loved that song so much, and it represented so perfectly the type of person he was—the kind who would "clap along if you know what happiness is to you"—that it was fitting to play it at his memorial service to remind everyone just who Sean was and why we all can learn so much about life from his penchant for happiness.

10

BE PASSIONATE AND PERSISTENT

As I write this chapter, I have a strong feeling of dread. Although I have never failed at anything up to this point, I am aware that when it comes to writing a book, I don't know what the hell I'm doing. Writing a book is hard, and I worry that I can't do it. Then I remember that Sean wouldn't quit something just because it's hard. Everything was hard for him, but that didn't stop him.

Usually I'm a very persistent person—maybe that's a gene I passed on to Sean. I started my company Nelligan Sports Marketing in 1999; nine months later, in March 2000, the economy melted down and the stock market tumbled. The business world was in upheaval, and corporate America was cutting back on advertising and marketing budgets, the lifeblood of our new company. But I kept working every day as hard as I possibly could, which eventually paid off and made the company successful. Why? Because I was passionate about what I was doing, and I wasn't going to give up.

The question for me now is: Am I passionate enough about writing this book to finish it? If I am, there's no question that I will follow the example of my hero, Sean, and keep at it, no matter how difficult.

NO PEP TALK NEEDED

In Sean's world, I saw over and over again that passion drives persistence. Nowhere was that more obvious than in his passion for sports—both as a player and a fan. One of his favorite sports was basketball, a sport that requires all the skills that Sean did not have: coordination, strength, speed, and agility. No matter. Sean loved basketball and wasn't going to give it up just because bocce (another sport he played and loved) was easier.

When Sean was about 12, I put a basketball hoop in our driveway. I knew he would love it, but what I didn't expect was that he would grab his coat in January and head out in 35-degree weather to practice. But he did, for hours.

My home office window faced the front of the house where I could see Sean in the driveway. I would watch him shoot and miss. Shoot and miss. Shoot and miss. Then I'd go out and rebound for him, trying to encourage him to keep at it. But he didn't need or want my encouragement. He would always insist, "I can do it myself." When I bought him a smaller ball to help him succeed, he wanted no part of that either. "I want the real thing," he'd say. No shortcuts for him. Sean never took the easy way or gave up just because something was hard. And he was right. Eventually, he became really good at putting the ball in the hoop. Using his signature one-handed 1950s set shot, he even scored 20 points in one of his games with his team, Storm. That's what persistence can do.

For Sean, failure wasn't an excuse for quitting. It was a reason to try harder. I never had to give him a pep talk to get back out there and try again. He would always try once more with the full confidence that one of these days he would make his shot. He had no fear of failure because he was used to that. It was a part of every task.

Maybe his friendship with failure is the reason Sean became so successful. Parents of mainstream children often tell me that they can't get their kids to persist at anything. Once something becomes hard, tiring, or frustrating, they quit. Many of these parents are aware that this is a kind of learned helplessness. Some kids quit because everything they've done before this difficult task has been easy. They have always won the prize. They got trophies just for showing up. They learned to expect instant success. When that doesn't happen, these kids can't keep trying.

Examples of this I-give-up trend are easy to find, but young kids are not the only ones losing the ability to seek out challenges and put in the work needed to be successful. In our instant-gratification, technology-driven world, adults also too often lose the ability to persist at something they feel passionate about.

In my own life, I struggle to measure up to the passion and persistence I saw every day in my son.

Sean and his cousins getting ready to go to a Taylor Swift concert at MetLife Stadium.

A SPECIAL KIND OF LOVE

Sean was light, love, and hope to everyone around him. He overcame so much and still chose the kind of love that doesn't make snap judgments and keeps no record of wrongs. Sean didn't sweat the little things; he just loved. That is the kind of love that I want to always carry with me. God's love was clearly present in who Sean was, and I am so thankful for the memories I have.

—Cousin Hailey Bryant

WHAT DOES YOUR TEAM LOOK LIKE?

Sean's gift of being passionately persistent also emerged in the way he taught himself how to be an informed sports fan, despite the fact that he couldn't read or calculate numbers. When Sean was about 22, I read that the iPad had apps that were helpful for special-needs kids. So I got him one and loaded it up with learning apps and also with sports apps. He especially loved the ESPN and Major League Baseball apps and would open them up and point at each team logo asking, "Who is that team?" "Who is this team?" over and over for hours.

Sean wanted to be able to identify the teams. He wanted to know what every college and major league team "looked" like by memorizing their logos. For college basketball he recognized the eye-patched pirate of Seton Hall and the red block "R" of Rutgers; in the National Football League he knew the blue, white, and red "NY" of the Giants; the green and white "G" of the Green Bay Packers; and the pirate flag of the Tampa Bay Buccaneers. It took hours, days, weeks, and months of persistent study and memorizing, but Sean never gave up.

Then during basketball season when he was 23 years old, we were sitting in my living room in Hoboken, New Jersey, watching college basketball as the ESPN scores were scrolling along the bottom of the TV screen. I could have fallen off my seat when Sean suddenly announced who was playing whom that day. I hit replay to check what he was saying. He had every one right.

Although this seemed like an amazing, almost impossible accomplishment for him, it really wasn't. What if you or I dedicated that much time to learning one thing, maybe a new language or a new skill like painting or cooking? There's no way we wouldn't master it eventually. But most of us don't. We get distracted or pulled in some other directions. We get bored. Lose interest. Move on.

Not Sean. When he was passionate about something, he was also persistent.

Sean winning gold in bocce at the 2014 Special Olympics USA Games.

IMPACT LIKE NO OTHER

Sean was a person of power and influence. Those are terms usually reserved for corporate presidents and CEOs, political figures and community leaders. But Sean's power was demonstrated by how he could change a room with the brilliance of his smile. His influence was profound through his words and unique perspective of life. Maybe it was communicated through his charm and sincerity or even his pure innocence, but, always, his presence could impact a room like no other.

—Marc. S. Edenzon, former President and Managing Director, Special Olympics North America

HOW MUCH IS SEVEN PLUS A TOUCHDOWN?

Not one to be content with this accomplishment, Sean then wanted to know the game scores. Although he knew most numbers, he got mixed up with double digits. But his desire to keep up on his sport teams pushed him to sit for hours on game day while I stood by the TV, like a teacher at the board in a classroom, pointing to the scores and asking, "What is this number? Which number is bigger? Who has the higher score?"

Then one afternoon, when Sean was 24, he was sitting on my couch and watching the college basketball scores scroll by, when he said, "Seton Hall beat Rutgers, and Georgia beat Michigan." I was stunned. How could he know that? He couldn't read, and I still didn't think he could do math. So how did he know that Georgia beat Michigan?

He had learned what I call "sports math," and his persistence continued. If I asked him what 7 plus 7 was, he wouldn't know. But when watching a football game that was tied at 7, he would say, "One more touchdown, and it will be 14 to 7. And if they get the field goal, it'll be 17 to 7." Baseball math worked the same way. Sean couldn't tell you what 3 times 1 was, but he knew that if there were two men on base when Aaron Judge hit a home run, the score would be 3 to 0. Tonight, as I was watching the Yankees in the 2019 postseason playoffs against the Astros, I heard Sean in my head, as clear as could be, informing me that if Aaron Hicks hits a home run with two men on, the Yankees would be winning 4 to 1. (And Hicks did hit the home run, just as Sean would have predicted.)

Sean had intellectual disabilities that made us assume he could never read sports scores, never mind calculate what the score would be after the next home run. I don't know what brain connections allowed him to juggle sports numbers without being able to add, subtract, or multiply, but I do know that there's a lesson in this for all of us.

Live Like Sean

What are you passionate about? For most of my adult life, I couldn't answer that question. I wanted to make a lot of money, and I worked hard at that. But that's not really the same thing as having enough intellectual curiosity to remove all the barriers that stand in the way of enjoying something I'm passionate about, no matter what other people assume I can't do.

People with "normal" intelligence are too often passive consumers of information. We don't need to work to get the news and certainly, as a general rule, don't have to be proactive in finding information. It comes to us. Google knows who the sport fans are from search histories and sends them lineups, scores, and highlight news. The evening news tells us what's important in the world based on the agenda of that news source. But Sean was not plugged into passive streams of information. When you can't read or multiply, you have to be pretty creative to figure out how to proactively get the knowledge you seek. To live like Sean, try to weave these actions into your life:

- Set your own agenda and goals without caring what's trending today.
- Seek out information for yourself, instead of relying on a news feed that strokes your predetermined interests.
- When logic—and friends—say you can't do something, but you feel passionately about what you're doing and are willing to persist, don't listen to the naysayers.
- Work hard to reach your goal. And then work even harder, no matter how long it takes or how slow your progress.
- Don't use failure as an excuse for quitting. Use it as a reason to try harder.

Sean showed me how to do all these things. It is his memory that guides the question I have to ask myself when faced with a difficult task: Do I have enough passion invested in this project to give it my all? Can I focus all my energies on its completion, even when I feel discouraged?

As I work on finishing this book, I can say that the answer to those questions is yes. I know that I will eventually hold the final manuscript in my hand, because I am learning how to live like Sean.

11

BE AN INSPIRATION

We all need role models to show us what is possible.

Who has inspired you? Who has encouraged you by example to be more, to be better? Who can you point to and say: "I want to be like that person"? Maybe it is an ancestor who bravely took the risk of leaving a homeland to emigrate to America expecting a better life. Maybe it is a friend who stared down a terrible illness and found a way back to good health. Maybe it is someone who was unfairly knocked down but came back with grace and dignity. In each of these examples, the root of the inspiration is not in the outcome, but in the bravery, the tenacity, and the grace and dignity to forge ahead.

Those are the kinds of attributes that inspire us to do more with the life we've been given.

BEING INSPIRED AND INSPIRING OTHERS

In my life, that inspiring person has been Sean. In the beginning, I always thought I would have to teach him about the world, and then I woke up one day and realized he was actually teaching me what is most important in my life—kindness, love, family, and friends. He did it in a humbling way, by example. And that inspiring example touched not only me but also so many others.

Because Sean's personality, his actions, and big heart helped those he met see the value of the inner person, rather than the outer trappings of a person's job, expensive home, or clothing, others were inspired to get involved in organizations and activities that support people like him with intellectual and developmental disabilities. Yes, Sean's example changed people's lives. I know that each member of my entire extended family is a different person—a better person—because of Sean. Thanks to the insights that Sean gave us, we have taken on the responsibility and joys of encouraging and creating opportunities for inclusion and acceptance. And as we do this, we hope to inspire others to do the same.

My work as Chairman and CEO of the 2014 Special Olympics USA Games grew not only out of my love of Sean but also from my new understanding of the needs and the beauty of children and adults with special needs. If Sean had not come into my life, those games would not have been in New Jersey, and our athletes would not have their own training facility in Lawrenceville.

Sean's sisters, Moira and Meghan, were his buddies, supporters, and cheerleaders. And, in turn, they felt blessed to be a part of his world and to see that world through his eyes. Just knowing him inspired them to get involved in activities that help others with special needs reach their full potential.

Sean's love of sports inspired Meghan to work tirelessly to raise money for her brother's Special Olympics basketball team by creating a Unified basketball game with the boys' and girls' high school varsity teams. Today that game is in its seventh year at Morristown-Beard School in New Jersey, where she is an alumna.

Moira has made it her mission to become a counselor or therapist for special-needs children, so that she can use her amazing skills and love to help many more Seans over the course of her career.

Although Sean will no longer be a part of the Storm basketball team, his mom, Maggie, remains a steady supporter and cheerleader. Despite the emotional pain it must cause her, she has chosen to follow the example of her son. She will not walk away from his teammates but instead has accepted the task of completing and filing all necessary paperwork for the team her boy loved so much.

Even Sean's cousins have been inspired by Sean to get involved in programs for special-needs children. Molly, Mac, and Connor Strange-Boston founded the Unified Sports track program in their high school in Ashland, Virginia. Mac got his fellow NJROTC cadets at Patrick Henry High School to serve at Tim Tebow's Night to Shine prom—a formal dance for those with special needs—in the cool "Dude Station," where the uniformed cadets gave guys a shoeshine and where the girls got their hair done. Mac passed the torch to Connor and Molly, who now are bringing the program forward. Additionally, Molly is volunteering at Young Life Capernaum, a youth group for people with special needs.

Cousins Erin, Shannon, and Jack Himes worked with the Best Buddies program to help their peers understand children with special needs. Erin also took a college internship at the 2015 Special Olympics World Games in Los Angeles and worked on the social media content marketing team.

If Sean had not been born into our family, I doubt we would have done any of these things. It is solely because of his influence that this small group of people continue, in a positive way, to touch the lives of people who touch the lives of people who touch the lives of people. It is this ripple effect that is so powerful. It pushes me to want to be the kind of person who, like Sean, inspires others. But how?

Coach TJ McHugh, Sean, Coach Geri Fredericks, and Bobby Fredericks getting ready for a Storm basketball game.

ONE OF A KIND

Sean was truly one of kind; the world is a better place for having had him in it. He left an impression on everyone he met, and his lessons and smile will never be forgotten.

—Coach TJ McHugh

LETTERS OF INSPIRATION

Since Sean's death I have received many letters, cards, emails, and texts from family members, friends, and his Special Olympics teammates. It is clear after reading the emotional comments from each person that Sean had a positive effect on all of them—each in a unique way. Many mentioned that Sean was an inspiration to them and that they now aspire to be better people because of him. (Some of these letters are reprinted in the Appendix of this book.)

These letters have given me the answer to my question: *How can I be an inspiration to others?* If I can live like Sean in just a few of the many ways he walked through each day, I know I will inspire others to do the same. I have no doubt it can happen in my own life—and in yours.

Imagine if, starting today, we made a conscious effort to live like Sean. How different our lives would be. How different the world around us would be!

Live Like Sean

Each chapter in this book is built on the blueprint Sean gave us. The book doesn't cover everything there is to know about this remarkable boy, but it gives us a good start in our attempt to be better—to make the world better.

Remember:

Be Grateful: Give yourself the chance to actively and consciously look for moments to say "thank you," and let those small moments contribute to growing the hope for future happiness.

Be Present: Pay attention to this moment. This person. This activity. This moment is the one and only thing we have complete control over, and yet, too often, we waste the opportunity to give it our full attention.

Be Friendly: Be *genuinely* friendly. Make a connection. Share a smile, a hello, and a short but genuine conversation with neighbors, colleagues, forgotten friends, strangers, kings, and paupers.

Be a Good Friend: Be the glue that holds your friendships together by being supportive and encouraging, honest and accepting, loyal and forgiving.

Be Loud: Know who you are. Know whom you love. And don't worry so much about what others think.

Be Brave: When the big picture is too difficult to handle, just put one foot in front of the other. If you bravely choose to make a change in your life, don't overthink what will happen in the next 20 years. Go for it. Sean didn't get another 20 years, and he didn't get the chance to make major life decisions.

Be Proactive: Banish the "can't" mindset from your life. Decide to achieve something and take one step at a time, no matter how small, then keep walking. Set goals that will bring you further along your life journey. Walk tall, proud, and happy.

Be Accepting: Learn to accept all people—with or without disabilities—with charitable judgment. If the person has a kind heart, accept them. In the end, that is all that matters.

Be Happy: Do not wait for your happiness to come through some accomplishment in the future. Bring it into your life each day, and strive to be happy for other people without jealousy or comparison. If you keep your heart open to the possibility of finding happiness in your daily interactions with other people, happiness will find a way inside you.

Be Passionate and Persistent: When logic—and friends—say you can't do something, don't listen if you feel passionately about what you're doing and are willing to persist. Don't use failure as an excuse for quitting. Use it as a reason to try harder.

If you can make even just a few of these "like-Sean" actions a part of your life, you will be a happier person and an inspiration to others. And that is world-changing.

APPENDIX

LETTERS OF LOVE

The letters that follow were written by people whose lives have been deeply touched by their relationship with Sean. Some are addressed to Sean; others are to me. All the writers have agreed to have their letters reprinted in this book, and I thank each one for being willing to publicly open their hearts and share their love of Sean.

Dear Sean,

It's me, Grandma. As I write this, it's been six-and-a-half long months since you went to heaven. I really miss you and still have trouble believing you are no longer here. Now that you have been with Jesus for this long, how are you doing? Is it really as overwhelming as we have believed? Can't believe you are there before us.

Papa Tim and I both learned so much from you. First, I loved our summer dinner and show probably as much as I ever could. I learned that I enjoyed seeing the play from your viewpoint. The story was always good, but it was the way you laughed, were sad, and reacted to the show that reached me. I remember you told me not to make a lot of noise or interrupt the actors because that might upset the other people at the play. You then laughed at a good part and asked me if I thought it was funny. Your laugh was from your toes to your eyes and made me enjoy your reaction more than anything.

You had a way of giving all your attention to me while we were eating. I thought about that and realized you knew a lot about what I liked, and you always tried to include that in conversation. Like at Christmas when you would ask what did I want for a gift. You asked what singers I liked. What songs, etc. I loved the fact that you liked "Aba Daba Honeymoon" and always asked me to sing it, and then you would laugh really hard.

Sean, you took the time to know what everyone liked and had an interest in and really listened to each person. This is something that you did very well. Like you, I am now trying to be present to whomever I am talking to. At the memorial, I heard your McMorrow cousin say how you learned what he liked, since it was not sports. He felt very good because you took the time to find out what was important to him so you could include that in your conversations and make him feel good about himself.

Sure love you,

Grandma Helen Nelligan

Dear Sean,

I want to start off by saying "thank you" for everything you have done for me. I know as your basketball coach it was my job to teach you, but it turns out the roles were reversed, and I have learned more from you than anyone could ever imagine. You are one of the most inspirational people I have had the pleasure of meeting, and your lessons will never be forgotten.

You always had a smile on your face and were always ready for some teasing and fooling around. We might have had the worst loss a basketball team could have, but you would always be positive. It didn't matter if you missed every shot you took during a game, you would be happy just running up and down the court. And when you did score, your excitement and smile lit up the world.

You taught me not to take life too seriously because there was always something positive that could be found (even when the Patriots were playing in the Super Bowl). Some of my happiest moments were hanging out with you. Whether it was in Wildwood during the state tournament, at the Devils game with the Storm team, or just a normal day at practice, you always knew how to make someone happy.

Thank you, Sean, for always being yourself. You truly are one of a kind; the world is a better place for having had you in it. And thank you for being a friend. You have left an impression on everyone you met, and your lessons and smile will never be forgotten.

Thank you,

Coach TJ McHugh

TJ,

Sean was pure goodness. He didn't have a mean bone in his body. If you were kind to Sean, he immediately embraced you and you became a friend for life. He had a great memory—just like you, his dad—for faces and names. I think it made people feel special that Sean always remembered them.

Sean taught me that children with disabilities are like all other children and have all the same needs and wants. They yearn to be treated like everyone else. Sean didn't know his limitations and was very happy with his abilities, which were the important ones. He knew right from wrong and would call someone out if they weren't being "nice." He would actually say, "That's not nice. You need to apologize." He had such a kind soul and didn't like to ever see anybody hurting.

What always amazed me about Sean was his pure honesty and his inability to tell a lie, even a little white lie. If you asked him something that he didn't want to answer or if he didn't want to tell you the truth, he either wouldn't answer you or would change the subject. Even for something as simple as after he'd come out of the bathroom, I'd ask, "Did you wash your hands?" And he'd just stare at me, and then say, "Oh, man," and go back to do it, even though he did not want to. He totally wanted to lie, but he just couldn't. Most kids would easily say, "Yes," and keep running by you to continue whatever they were doing.

He also would just blurt out, "You're very nice, Dana. I love you. You're a very nice person." I can hear him saying that as I type this. I'll miss that. He made everyone feel special and knew when you needed to hear things like that.

Even with more complex subjects, Sean knew what to keep separate in his life. He lived a sort of dual life: one with you and me, and one with his mom and sisters. He was very careful to censor what he said or share about what he'd been up to. We found it interesting that he was capable of making this distinction. We used to always say that he knows so much more than we think he does. It often made us laugh while watching TV when he'd burst out laughing at sarcasm or some adult joke. I believe Sean understood so much more than we knew, and I find peace knowing that he's finally able to express himself wholly with no restrictions.

Sean was a bright light in an often busy, stressed-out world. He taught me to slow down and appreciate all the little things we often take for granted. Tell people you care about them and compliment them often. Even months later, everyone still asks me about Sean and how we are all doing because he left such a huge impression on everyone he ever met. Rest in peace, Sean. You are missed every day.

Dana Nelligan

Dear Sean,

Thank you. Thank you for showing me how to love so well and to live without judgment. Jesus calls us to show others his unconditional love; I can't begin to describe how well you did that. From your endless smile, a contagious laugh, and your big bear hugs that were never long enough, even though some would last two minutes. You lit up the room with love but never wanted all the attention. You saw only the good in people, which I think is so beautiful, because as people got to know you, they realized there was only good in you. You taught me so much. I can only hope I love people as much as you loved all of us. Actually, I don't think that's possible, but I'll try every day.

Love,

Connor Strange-Boston

Dear Uncle TJ,

I was studying abroad in 2014 and missed the Special Olympics National Games in New Jersey. I was really jealous of my whole family as they came together to watch Sean compete. So in 2015, when the Special Olympics World Games were set to be in Los Angeles, I knew I had to be a part of it.

I applied for an internship and worked all summer long on the content marketing team, writing blogs and telling stories of athletes from all corners of the world as they prepared to compete on the biggest stage. I spent the week of the games at UCLA, working with a team of volunteers to find all of the most inspiring and incredible moments of the games and capture them. It was not only the most formative experience of my professional career but also one of the most inspirational and exciting events I have ever experienced.

These experiences have shaped the course of my life, and I simply wouldn't have found them without Sean's influence. What truly impacted me the most deeply was just knowing and loving Sean. His positive attitude was contagious, the way he loved his family was heartwarming, and his honesty was so refreshing. Being around him made all of us better, because he was simply himself at all times.

But the ways he impacted me are just a small part of his story. I see the same things in all of my cousins, in my aunts and uncles and grandparents, in every friend of Sean's I've met and interacted with. Each and every person he knew is better because of him. He was a light and made those around him feel good, and he inspired me to live a bit more fearlessly and honestly. To live like Sean means to live passionately, to see the best in people, and to live honestly and truthfully, and I'll spend the rest of my life trying to emulate him in those ways.

Erin Nelligan Himes

Sean,

You are the epitome of God's love and grace. The Bible tells us that we are all made in God's image, but to me you looked a little more like Him than the rest of us. He used you and the influence He gave you to give everyone you came into contact with a glimpse of hope, love, and truth. There is not a judgmental bone in your body. You just wanted to love everyone on a deep level. I remember being so refreshed after every conversation that we had because you were so intentional and genuinely cared about how I was doing. I can honestly say that I know Jesus better because I knew you, Sean. I know you're probably in heaven right now, telling God what the score of the Giants game will be with amazing accuracy and performing your amazing dance moves for Him when you get the score right. Thank you for showing me what it's like to love unconditionally. I love you!

I'll see you soon, big guy.

Your cousin,

Mac Strange-Boston

Dear TJ,

I remember the day I learned I was going to be an aunt for the first time, and I remember commuting with you and Maggie to New York City while Maggie was pregnant! I was so excited. I also remember the moment the phone rang letting us know you both were on the way to the hospital to have the baby. I was ready to go too, but was told by Mom that I was to wait; it wasn't my place to be there. Damn. I thought this was gonna be my child, too. But she was right, and I stayed and waited.

I was so proud of having Sean as my nephew and godson! I loved holding him, feeding him, and even changing his diaper. When Sean was about three months old, you and Maggie went for a getaway, and I got to babysit. I couldn't wait. (Thankfully, I was still living with Mom and Dad, because I was gonna need help!) I took Sean to the Fourth of July parade and celebration in our hometown. It was part of our upbringing, and I was so excited to show him everything and show him off to everyone we knew. I also remember having to go back home after about two hours because he had drooled and pooped through every outfit I brought for him, but I brought him right back and showed him off some more.

I didn't know at that time that he was a child with special needs, or at least I don't remember knowing. Maybe I was in denial, but I knew my job was to love him unconditionally, and I did! As a matter of fact, I don't remember ever being told that Sean had special needs or that he was differently abled, although I am sure I was told at some point. All I remember was loving every minute of watching him grow and learn. And that's just it. Until the day Sean unexpectedly left us, he was still learning and growing. He was amazing.

There were little things that started to appear that showed Sean wasn't right on track to meet his milestones. He definitely struggled to do anything that required strength. When our sister had a baby a month after Sean was born, it became obvious after a while that they weren't on the same track of development. I admired how you and Maggie did all the right things, took him to all the right doctors and therapists, and I know that was not easy. When Sean was about one, I moved far away and only saw him every couple of months and was always greeted with a smile and willingness to play and laugh. Seeing Sean always kept life in perspective.

Love you,

Sheila Nelligan Himes

Dear TJ,

A letter of this magnitude is difficult and should never have to be written. I have written so many drafts, I have lost count. Each day since June 16 I think of Sean, and you, the girls, and Maggie, and Dana. Each day I pray for peace and hope for all of you. Each day, I cry and my heart aches, and I feel so much pain. I know it's nothing compared to your loss. I hope, in a small way, knowing how much Sean is loved and will always be loved by so many helps a little. To be honest, I still cannot even believe it is true.

The only thing that gets me through is knowing without a doubt that Sean is in heaven with Jesus and the God that created him for such a life. God knew what He was doing when He created Sean. I am so very grateful that He placed Sean in our family. He selected the perfect parents for Sean, and TJ, the perfect son for you. Together you were quite a team. A team that has influenced so many people for the better, and continues to do so. Sean brought a lot of gifts to the table. Sean's amazing life, albeit way too short, will continue to influence people for generations.

Sean was a magnet. Everyone was attracted to him because he made others feel good, naturally, without trying. At every Nelligan gathering everyone would vie to be next to Sean, to spend time with Sean, to speak with him, dance with him, to get a selfie with him, to laugh and joke around with him, to hug him, and tell him how much he is loved. Sean inevitably would turn the tables and ask how we were doing, and joke with us, and laugh at our attempts to be funny and, of course, to share a big hug. The thing with Sean is he did all of that so much better than any of us could. Sean didn't expect or demand attention. He was charismatic and a giver and in turn attracted the attention he so rightly deserved. Sean came by these traits naturally, and they were enhanced by being in an environment that included others who cared deeply for him and others with special needs (you, Maggie, Moira, Meghan, and Dana, and those you placed around him). Sean was able to become the best he could be because of it.

This letter cannot capture how much I love Sean or how much he has influenced my life, because I am still learning about that as we move forward without him (here on earth). He is and will always be in my heart.

Here's some of what I know today . . . how Sean influences me and my family:

I remember the call the hotel operator put through to my hotel room in Quito, Ecuador, on April 10, 1990. Imagine all the communication we had to do, before cell phones and texting, for you to know where I would be on the day Sean was born. The day that changed everything for our family. Sean made you parents, Mom and Dad grandparents, and the rest of us aunts/uncles. We are a kid family, so to say I was excited to be an aunt is an understatement. You know it's a significant person and event when you can recall the date and exactly where you were at the moment you first heard the great news. Little did we know Molly Kate would be born 13 years later to the date, to round out the cousin clan and become the cousin "bookend" to Sean. Molly holds this title close to her heart. She is always proud to tell everyone she and Sean share a birthday because it makes her feel so special.

I was babysitting Sean for the weekend at your first house in Montville. Sean was about four years old. We were playing some sort of game where running around the living room was in order, according to Sean. Being a young special education teacher at the time, I was secretly working on two-step instructions during this game, none of which Sean wanted anything to do with. I was trying hard, and he was laughing hysterically. Then, all of a sudden, he stopped; he turned around and looked at me. We gazed at each other, smiling, knowingly. I finally said with a grin, "You understand every single thing I'm saying to you, don't you?" The twinkle in his eyes and giggle confirmed it. We laughed together and continued playing, this time with no rules, just running around having fun! Sean knew how to have fun. He influenced the way I spoke with my students, who were deaf, thereafter, and how I presented information and communicated with them. I always gave them the benefit of the doubt, believing they understood me, and I know they appreciated this. It's just respectful.

I remember the Special Olympics NJ state games where Sean marched out onto the field while you served as the emcee announcing the teams and volunteers. I can still see Sean walking out with his team with a giant smile, coming around the curve on the right side of the track, giving high fives to everyone. I remember Mac, a toddler at the time, getting sweaty in the stands because he was dancing so furiously to the beat of the music blasting and telling everyone that Sean was his cousin. I was so proud to be your sister and Sean's aunt, and Mac was so proud to be Sean's cousin and your nephew! Looking back, it was like Sean's "coming of age party." He was about to bust loose and so were you! The tide was changing. The ripple effect began. Sean's influence . . .

I would often "lose" Connor when he was little, because he "was a runner" much like Sean, if you recall. When Connor was about three years old, I "lost" him at Timmy's soccer game. I began to panic but thought to myself, where would he be, what attracts him? I looked for something yellow, as he was obsessed with yellow at the time. I looked around and, yup, there he was in the middle of a buttercup field. Later at the Special Olympic USA games, Connor wandered off while collecting state pins. He was older (12), but I got worried. I thought once again, where would he be? What attracts him? I looked for Sean and, yup, there was Connor just hanging out with Sean and his friends, kicking back in the shade just sitting together.

Watching Connor create the wall hanging for Sean made from the SOUSA 2014 T-shirt and the pins he and Molly collected was so touching. He made it by himself and did not want any help. It hangs now in Connor's bedroom as a very special reminder of his relationship with Sean. Sean's influence . . .

When we came home from SOUSA 2014, Mac began the work to create a Unified track team at his high school, an idea that was promoted at the games. He scheduled a meeting between his high school administration and Special Olympics Virginia. To say it took persistence is an understatement. Change is never easy. Mac was not deterred. He recruited one of his best friends and a supportive teacher, and they tackled it together. In 2014, they held their first UniPHied track meet. Six years later, the team is still in full force. Connor and Molly are on the team and have helped to recruit the next generation of track team members. Sean's influence . . .

Mac recruited his fellow NJROTC cadets to serve at Tim Tebow's Night to Shine prom RVA. They created the "Dude Station," where the uniformed cadets provide shoeshines to the male participants, while the girls get their hair done. Our favorite part was that Mac and one of his best friends, who happens to have special needs, also a cadet, served alongside one another giving shoeshines before hitting the dance floor all night. Mac passed the torch to the younger cadets at his high school, and they continue to organize the Dude Station, year after year. Sean's influence . . .

These are but a few of the ways that Sean has influenced me and my children. When I think about Sean, I am overcome with a feeling of love, and I immediately think about how I need to be more like Sean. Sean taught me how to have more fun, be in the moment more, know that each encounter matters, accept others as they are, respect all, and love big. Love, the greatest of all things.

Sean is without a doubt happy in heaven and sharing joy with others, as he always did. I miss him so much. To have lived a life like Sean's is an amazing thing. His influence is deep and wide and will continue on long into the future.

Until we meet again, and we will. I love you, Sean!

I love you, TJ.

Terri Nelligan

To the reader,

"You're only as happy as your unhappiest child."

I've repeated that quote often in my life—talking to friends or family about our kids and their day-to-day challenges. And while I really believe that it's true, I've been lucky enough to have healthy and happy kids with the normal ups and downs of growing up. When I think back to when Sean was younger and it became evident that he would have permanent disabilities, I remember some of the things TJ and Maggie were worried about and grieving. TJ has talked about one particular appointment with a world-renowned neurologist and how devastated they were to hear his predictions of all the limitations Sean would face in his lifetime. He grieved the loss he felt, understanding that he wouldn't coach Sean's little league team or teach him to drive. He worried about how Sean would fit in and if he'd suffer socially and be ultimately unhappy realizing his limitations.

Well, any parent would have to grieve and process that

information as best they could. Some would probably give up. Some might end up doing everything for that child so they didn't have to face failure or be sad. Some would be angry and not be able to move past the misfortune. However, it seemed to take TJ and Maggie no time at all to realize that Sean was anything but a "misfortune." Sean wasn't sad about what he couldn't do. He was happy for what he could do. He tried everything he was presented with and smiled the whole time. I wonder if part of my brother's initial grief was worrying that his son would not be happy.

Sean thrived over the years—in school, at work, at sports, and most especially at winning hearts. He surpassed many of the milestones expected of him, largely because of his attitude, because many things were difficult for him. It was his God-given nature to be happy and to persevere, and to love. We should all respect, admire, love, and honor that attitude. That spirit. That love and most especially that smile, which was so infectious. We should live like Sean. We should be grateful for all that we have and live in the moment. He did just that.

But there is another very important component to recognize and a lesson to garner for anyone reading this important book. Sean's nature was certainly to love and persevere and smile and laugh. But he was also nurtured and encouraged and was never held back from accomplishing whatever he could. My brother and his wife grieved for their son and his future when they were confronted with the realities of Sean's limitations. They were sad . . . we all were. However, they got up and reset their sights on giving Sean a full and wonderful life within his new and accepted abilities and limitations. They signed him up for Special Olympics and supported him at every sport he played; they volunteered at his school for people with special needs; they hosted fundraisers for the school; they brought him and his new friends to see concerts and spent countless hours watching all of his favorite sports. When he was older, he worked at TJ's college sports marketing company and restaurant, learning more skills and getting along wonderfully with his coworkers, who loved him. He accompanied my brother to dinners with his buddies, and eventually Sean felt they were his buddies, too. TJ often called him the Mayor, as he was so comfortable with adults and hanging out talking shop about his favorite teams.

TJ and Sean could often be seen on TV behind home plate at a Yankees game, and they braved the cold watching the Giants play live. His sisters stood proud and loved and protected him fiercely. Sean was included in every single thing they did as a family and was taught how to be loving and accepting and kind. In turn, we all learned vital lessons about not giving up and being present and grateful and kind.

Sean had a beautiful disposition, and we all loved being around him. When he got older, he became more social and would strike up conversations. The last time I saw him, he was quick to ask, "How's Allie?" (my oldest daughter). He also had a great sense of humor and loved to be teased. He was a remarkable judge of character, so if you were with someone he wouldn't talk to, you'd likely consider what that person was hiding!

Live like Sean. What an incredible tribute to an amazing young man who overcame so many obstacles to be happy with life. But I'll add we should also live like my brother, Sean's mom and sisters, and every other parent who gives their special-needs child support to try new things, who hold their heads high at sporting events or concerts or in restaurants, proud of their loving sons and daughters and refusing to let anyone judge them for the things they can't do.

Live like my brother, who redirected his goals as a father, rose above his grief for the son he thought he'd have, and loved the one he did have. Unconditionally. He'll tell you he loved Sean unconditionally because Sean was so capable of unconditional love himself. And I believe that's true. But what came first?

Sean was born into a family of people who never shied away from pushing him to be all that he could be, from encouraging him to do things he may have been reluctant to try. They never shied away from including his friends in family activities, from cheering him on at basketball, bocce ball, and his other Special Olympics triumphs. He was included in everything. Loved like crazy. Taken care of. Given the opportunity to thrive. And in return we all learned lessons about love and life.

Sean will be missed by all of us forever. We will strive to remember to live like him. But I for one will also strive to live like TJ as well.

Eileen Nelligan Corcoran

Sean,

When you were a baby, the doctors said that you likely would never walk. We have said time and time again that you proved them wrong, but I think in some sense they were right. You were never made to walk through life. You were born to run! You overcame nearly every obstacle that was put in your path, and you did it with greatness. You went to school, had multiple jobs, played as many sports as you could, and even played in the national games of the Special Olympics! You had more friends than anyone could ever ask for, and you never saw differences or disabilities but just loved everyone equally. This world could stand to have a lot more people like you in it!

Your love for and knowledge of sports were always amazing to me. You never let a question about how you were doing or what you wanted for Christmas go without answering and then immediately you'd counter with, "You?"

One of my favorite memories with you was going to the

Taylor Swift concert. We danced, sang, and you reminded me all night that you, me, and Taylor are all the same age. You loved to dance! At my wedding, I found myself stopping to watch you dance several times, because the joy it brought you was contagious. There could have been no one else on the dance floor, and you would've been out there dancing your heart out. I had hoped to one day go to a Yankees vs. Orioles game with you and your dad and bring Bradley along. His love for baseball reminds me of you. We would've cheered for the Os, and you would've said "Boo!" and cheered for the Yankees. But, one day we will make it to a game, and I know you'll be there watching with us from the best seat in the house. Maybe Rob will even root for the Yankees just for you.

Though I will never truly understand why you had to leave this life so soon, I have to believe that God had much bigger plans for you than anyone here on earth could have predicted. We are all better for knowing you.

Love and miss you always!

Your cousin,

Allie Himler

Dear TJ,

As you know, I work with a lot of very challenging people every day. Most of them have much different backgrounds than I do. It is so easy to judge when they do or say something I find offensive. I have thought about Sean so much lately when I work with those whom people might judge for a variety of reasons—being dirty, obese, mean to nurses, dementia, addiction, etc. I am finding that, because of Sean, I am much more accepting of everyone. I still process some of those negative thoughts but try to replace them with compassion and by talking to people without judging them. It is interesting to see how people react when they are used to being judged and then suddenly are treated with respect.

I know Sean never judged anyone. He just accepted and loved everyone. I have a long way to go to match that, but I'm working on it!

Kristi Nelligan

DESI'S TOP TEN FAVORITE "SEAN THINGS"

1. *I love the way that Sean was always happy and smiling.*
2. *I like that Sean played soccer with us at Storm.*
3. *I like that Sean made jokes in the car. He laughed a lot.*
4. *I like that Sean went with us to the flower show.*
5. *I like that Sean went to Midland.*
6. *I like that Sean played basketball.*
7. *I like that we went to a museum with Sean, and we played games there and we had a great time.*
8. *I like that Sean liked dogs.*
9. *I like that Sean watched Friends on TV.*
10. *Sean was a great friend.*

Desi Cleary, a teammate of Sean's for basketball and soccer, who went to the Midland School with him.

TJ,

I talked to my daughter, Theresa; she is limited in her ability to understand detailed information, but she was very, very sad when we lost Sean. She remembered him as always kind to her, very quiet but supportive. I have many pictures of her with him at soccer and track/field and basketball games, and he was always standing near her. He was a great support for her when she was new to the team.

I remember that Theresa was very nervous about joining the all-boys team when she was 15 years old. I pushed her to join, as I wanted to open up new doors for her. Both Sean and Bobby welcomed her warmly to the team, and Sean's quiet support was very comforting to Theresa. He often sat next to her and would put his arm around her with a quick hug. I think Theresa, as the only girl, felt very overwhelmed at times, and she had to prove her own skills to the entire team before they would even hand her the ball. It was a slow road for her to earn the respect of this all-boys team. But Bobby and Sean both embraced her and gave her a chance.

Sean was forever smiling, and I know Theresa loved that; it gave her more confidence, and she found it encouraging. The icing on the cake was at the last fundraising game at Morristown-Beard. During one of the final scrimmages, Sean had the ball and shouted Theresa's name, and when she turned to look, he actually passed her the ball. In all the years I have seen them play, Sean would only do a quick close-by pass, but that time he gave it a powerful throw across the gym to Theresa. Later she said to me, "Did you see Sean passed me the ball?" She was so happy and even thrilled that he would pass to her. We all miss Sean.

Carol Pede Pedoto

Dear Sean,

When I starting teaching, I knew I would meet many great students, and they would all impact my life in some way. Sean, you found a very special place in my heart. Before you joined my class, we already had a connection. All you had to do was smile and say hi. You had this way of making everyone want to be around you. I don't know how many times you asked me, "What did you have for dinner?" We all knew that was your way to communicate your interest in people and your way to be heard.

The year you joined my super senior class was when we really got to know each other. We developed a special bond in many ways. You made me laugh on a daily basis, and nothing was better than when I got you to laugh and smile that big smile of yours. It washed away any daily stress I had.

We connected with sports. I cannot go to a Giants game without remembering when we met in the parking lot, or remember our Mets vs. Yankees rivalry. Our favorite show was American Idol. We truly connected with the traditions we began and the communication skills that you developed, using that show to talk with so many people. One of my best memories was the night I went to your house for the American Idol finale party with your family. I got to see a very loving family who had made the night special and fun.

No words can truly express how I feel now, but I do know I am one lucky teacher. I was the one who was blessed to have you in my class and now in my heart for the rest of my life.

Thank you for our special connection! I will think of you often.

With love,

Kathy Tauscher

(Sean's teacher at the Midland School)

Dear Sean,

Each day when I sit down at the desk in my office, I see a picture taken a few years back that includes you, me, Liam, and baseball icon Don Zimmer. This was a special day, as we were on the field at Yankee Stadium before the game. At one point, we were all sitting in the dugout just taking in the scene, thinking how surreal and lucky we were to be there. For me, this is just one of the many great memories that your friendship gave me and my family. More important than these great memories, though, are the lessons you instilled in all of us. Lessons that far exceed some friends attending big events. Lessons that are best defined as "unconditional."

When something is defined as unconditional, it means that it is absolute and not subject to any terms or conditions. No matter what the circumstances, it will happen and be constant. There is no other way or word to best describe who and what you were all about. You applied a high degree of "unconditional" to each and every one of your friends. You were not concerned with age, color, height, weight, or status. You did not form a friend hierarchy but rather treated each and every one of us with the same level of love and respect.

Thanks to your unconditional approach to life and friendships, we were all granted a front-row seat to what should be one of life's greatest and most important lessons. Through your exemplary actions, we all witnessed firsthand how people should be treated. They should be loved and respected regardless of the circumstances they are subject to. For this, we all owe you a big word of thanks.

While we all miss your big presence and especially that big smile, you have left us with many great memories. These memories will carry me, and all of us, forward, and each memory brings a smile to my face each time I think of the many events and journeys we made together. Our time together was always fun and filled with laughter. With and through you, we were all transported to a different world and place—centered on just the here and now. Because of you, we were transported to the unconditional world of Sean and had front-row seats to how life should be lived. You had the unique gift to make better each person that you came in contact with. For me specifically, you made me a better father, husband, friend, and most importantly a better person.

Thank you for the great memories.

Thank you for allowing me to be part of your life.

Thank you for your unconditional love and friendship.

Forever your friend,

Brian Mulhall

Dear Sean,

I want you to know that I think of you every day. I have a picture of you in my car that your Uncle Mike gave me. I want you to know that I miss you and would give anything to come see you play one more Sunday morning hoops game. Or just to hang with you and your dad and watch a Giants or Yankees game, so you could correct me all game long when I got every player's name wrong.

I still remember the last time that I saw you. We were together at the Montville Inn, and you asked me when you were going to see me again, and I told you very soon. I told you that I would miss you until I saw you again, and you looked at me and laughed and said, "You're a good guy, NickyBoy," and you gave me a big hug.

Looking back now, I wish I had stayed a little while longer that night and made more memories talking endlessly about the Giants and Yankees.

You were the happiest person I knew. You lit up every room you ever walked into and made a lasting impression on every person you ever met. I look at old pictures I have saved of our memories, but it's just not the same. But I know you are happy still. Every time I see your picture, I smile, and I hear you say, "NickyBoy."

I am blessed and honored to have had you as a friend.

I just wish I had just one more memory . . . I miss and love you, buddy!

Love,

Nick "NickyBoy" Matarazzo

Sean,

I miss going to your basketball games, to our Wiffle ball games on the beach, and on our attempted bike rides. (I know you liked to bike ride; you just didn't like to pedal!) I miss breakfast at the beach house while everyone else was sleeping, and going to every sports event imaginable with your dad. But most of all, I miss hanging out, watching TV, and making you laugh, and what I would give to hear you say just one more time, "You know. You know. Stop teasing, Duke. You're funny." I think about you every day and about how you taught us all what's really important. God bless.

Love and miss you,

Andrew Duke

Dear Sean,

I always believed that things happen for a reason. When Tom was hired at Nelligan Sports Marketing in 2001, never did I know how much my life would change forever. Fate brought us together. Not only did I meet your amazing dad and family, I also befriended you. At first you were shy and not very talkative. However, your enormous hugs said it all, and we started a friendship that would take us on many adventures and allow us to nourish our relationship.

I remember joining you at the Rutgers University vs. Ball State Bowl Game in Toronto. You and I watched from a private room. You emceed the game and knew the outcome at kickoff time: You called the win for our team. Then there were the days at the beach when we played games and went for bike rides. When it was time for the annual barbecue, it gave me such pleasure to see you enjoy the steak dinner and chocolate cake for dessert. You always complimented the chef (me). I think it was there that after a fun night you told me that I was a funny lady. I know that was the result of always being happy with you.

But most of all, you introduced me to Special Olympics. Each year my sixth graders learned about intellectual disabilities. The culminating activity was to accompany me to the opening ceremonies at TCNJ. The students had homemade banners and were excited to be a part of the games. We also cheered the athletes who participated in the skating events during the winter games. When I retired, many of the letters I received from them thanked me for teaching them what it meant to have a disability and how you can achieve anything. Volunteering during the 2014 National Games was another extraordinary experience. I was there to cheer you on and applauded your perseverance at every award ceremony. Standing with your loving family, who always provided you with love and support, was just as rewarding.

Because of you I am now volunteering at a place that provides young children and adults the opportunity to learn life skills like shopping, banking, visiting a doctor or dentist, going to a movie, buying popcorn, and much more. I call it my happy place, and wish you could have joined me there.

I don't know why you had to leave us, but I know how very much you are missed. Your infectious laughter always helped to make a dark day brighter. Your beautiful soul lives on forever, and the memories of you will be in my heart forever. You were very special to me.

I send my love up to heaven every day. I miss you.

Love,

Judy Varga

Dear Sean,

I remember the first time I met you. We were at the Brendan Byrne Arena in the Nelligan Sports Marketing suite for a Nets basketball game. TJ introduced us, and you barely looked up from your shoes. Over the next 19 years, I watched as you grew into the man who would light up a room just by walking in and saying "Hi, how ya doin'?"

I was working at Rutgers for Nelligan Sports when Greg Schiano began to build the football program. You became a big fan of Rutgers, and you knew how important it was to me for us to win. You always seemed to know what was important to someone. It was then that our tradition started that before the first Rutgers football game, I would give you the Rutgers football jersey of your current favorite player. I looked forward to this as much as you did.

We had such fun going to Rutgers home games, traveling to away games, bowl games, NCAA games, and Giants games.

I have many fond memories of our time together. I remember on one trip to Florida, to watch Rutgers and South Florida, TJ, you, and I were having dinner, and you looked at me and said, "Tommy"—you always called me Tommy—"we're going to lose tomorrow."

I said, "Sean, I think you are messin' with me."

You said, "Noooo," and you repeated this several more times during the evening. Then you would always say, "I'm just teasing, Tommy."

There was also one trip to West Virginia when we flew into Pittsburgh. It was a particularly windy fall day. Needless to say, it was a bumpy ride. In fact, the pilot tried to land the plane three times, and each time he had to abort and try again. TJ and I were looking at each other in terror with white knuckles, and you just laughed and had a ball. Maybe we should have tried that.

Soon after that I got introduced to Special Olympics because of your dad's involvement and your participation. My first event was attending the Special Olympics Summer Games at TCNJ. I remember your being sick just after I got there. You were very nervous about the experience. As the years went on and your participation grew, so did mine. After seeing how you grew at Special Olympics, I wanted to be involved and help others grow as well.

Then New Jersey won the bid to host the 2014 SOUSA Games, and your dad asked me to be part of the 2014 team. For three years our team worked to accomplish our goals, and that included changing the paradigm of how these games were organized. I was so pleased that we were successful in providing Special Olympics athletes from across the country the time of their lives. To see you win a medal in bocce was especially satisfying. I can safely say that those three years changed my life. Since the 2014 Games, I have become even more involved with SONJ and now serve as vice chair on the Board of Trustees. People always ask me how I got so involved in Special Olympics. My answer is always the same, "Sean recruited me!"

I also had the pleasure of being a work colleague of yours at Nelligan Sports Marketing. We always had a saying in the company that we didn't have a job, but rather we had a lifestyle. We were an NSM family, and when you and Bobby joined us on a regular basis to mail out invoices to hundreds of sponsors of our university partners, you became our family. You and Bobby always brightened our days in the office and reminded us every day what's important in life.

Sean, when I was young my mother had a friend with an intellectual disability. She would take several buses to get to our house to see my mother. At the time I never understood what the relationship meant to her. But Sean, now I do, and I believe there is a connection between then and now. You made me understand what it means to have that relationship with a person with intellectual disabilities.

Sean recruited me! I have a magnet on my desk with your picture with the saying, "Live Like Sean." I look at it every day and try to live like you. I miss you, buddy!

Tommy Varga

Sean,

Oh, Sean, you are so loved and will be forever missed for all the love you shared and the lessons you taught those who knew you.

I first met Sean on the day I began my teaching career at the Children's Center for Therapy and Learning, CCTL. It was September 15, 1997. He was a shy, skinny little seven-year-old with a big smile on his face, who was very quiet and very observant of everything going on around him, with an infectious laugh and a twinkle in his eyes. I knew I was going to love him instantly—teachers do that!! But not just Sean; he was only one in a class of nine wonderful kids, several who were to be with me for the next seven years. And what a bond we built with all those families!

Sean's mom, Maggie, was seven months along in her pregnancy with Meghan, and we were all so excited for Sean to be a big brother for the second time. Sister Moira was four. What a wonderful family Sean was part of. How happy and proud Sean was that day in November when, holding Daddy TJ's hand, he walked into class to show us all pictures of his new baby sister!

Sean's family was always involved in the life of my class, with birthday parties, holiday celebrations, volunteer readers, grandparents day, fundraisers for the school, any event we had. I learned very quickly that I could always count on their support. As a culmination to our summer program one year, we worked on a production of The Wizard of Oz, *under the guidance and creativity of Carol Barron, a personal assistant to one of the girls in our class who was nonverbal and wheelchair bound and who played Dorothy. Carol helped us adapt everything so all the kids could participate. Dress rehearsal went really well! As the families and guests gathered in our very crowded classroom the next day for our big performance, the excitement and anticipation was palpable. Sean had the role of the Cowardly Lion and looked adorable in his costume, as did his buddies. When it came time for Sean to join Dorothy, Michael as the Scarecrow, and Geoffrey as the Tin Man,* HE WOULDN'T LEAVE HIS SEAT! *It was hilarious, now as I look back on that day, but so like the shy guy he was at that time.*

Through the love that surrounded Sean as he grew and learned and experienced life, he became a true champion. People were drawn to Sean by his humor, his curiosity, and the unconditional love he shared with everyone.

As I mentioned earlier, I was Sean's teacher for seven years, as the CCTL transitioned to become the P.G. Chambers School. Sean's family was a very generous donor to the building fund as the program and school grew. They were just one of many families who recognized the wonderful education, physical therapy, occupational therapy, and speech/language therapy programs that continue to be a part of that organization, where all children, regardless of their different abilities, are encouraged to reach their fullest potential.

Because we grew, Sean was able to stay at the school until he was 14 and had to move on to a high school program. How difficult a transition that was for the students and parents, some of whom had been with the program since early intervention services and the preschool program. It was equally difficult on me, the teacher. It was like having four of your own children graduate and move on! But how blessed I was to have forged relationships with these very special children and their families. We became an extended family, a great support system to one another. Those bonds remain to this day. In fact, when I learned of Sean's sudden passing, I contacted as many of those families as I could find, many of whom were in attendance at the celebration of life that was held two weeks later.

For his high school program, Sean moved on to Midland School, where he continued to bloom with the support of other loving teachers and staff. At some point during his first year there, Maggie contacted me to see if I'd be interested in tutoring Sean for a couple of hours a week. She knew I was working with another former student, Tim Baird, who was a close friend of Sean's. I was thrilled to be able to help out.

We started out with some reading of functional words, improving letter formation, and some numbers work. I quickly took my lead from Sean and his fascination with numbers, the calendar, days of the week, times of day, etc. And he loved to eat, so we did cooking activities that required measuring and following recipes, which I could adapt for his needs. We also did some menu planning and would make a list of items needed for a recipe, and go to the grocery store, come home, and cook together. This all helped to develop life skills and model some appropriate public behaviors. Not that he was ever bad in the store, he just did some very silly things, and if you knew Sean, you know how he loved to make people laugh!

I also learned very quickly how many people Sean knew and how well known he was around town! Sometimes we'd go out to purchase a gift, a card, or stop at a restaurant so he could get a "snack," which was good practice in reading a menu. Rarely did we have an outing where Sean wasn't recognized or he found someone he knew to greet. Sean had great social skills and was always happy to shake a hand or give a big bear hug. He was no longer the shy, skinny little guy I met in September 1997. I remember running into Sean and Maggie in the pet supply store with my dear husband, Al, who had not been well. Sean immediately shook Al's hand and said, "How are you feeling, Al? You better?" Sean always cared about others, their health, and their feelings and loved them unconditionally.

I mentioned his fascination with numbers, and this was shown in his interest and amazing memory for people's birthdays. Of course, he always enjoyed a good celebration and parties! When Sean was about 16, we began a tradition of celebrating our April birthdays together, as they're only a week apart. This usually involved a restaurant trip, with Tim Baird joining the fun, as his birthday is in mid-March. What fun memories I have of dining out with these two amazing buddies! Sean liked to remind me that I wasn't his teacher anymore, but we were good friends. I don't know if he ever knew how truly special our relationship was, but I suspect he did!

Sean graduated from Midland in 2011, and I was included in all of the festivities and celebrations, as I had always been: birthdays, his First Holy Communion, family Halloween parties, to name a few. I had become part of his loving extended family and pray that will always be.

In 2013, after losing my husband to leukemia and becoming a grandma to a beautiful baby girl in North Carolina, it was time for me to move out of New Jersey. Even with 500 miles between us, we kept in touch. Maggie and I had become great friends and a support system for each other though many ups and downs and the transitions of life. Who knew how special we'd become to each other, but life has a way, and I believe God has a plan. Faith will keep us strong!

When I come back to visit in New Jersey, a visit to the Nelligans in Montville is always on my list. I often make my home base at Maggie's home. And a real treat is visiting the shore house on Long Beach Island. I remember taking Tim with me for a stay there! Not so long ago, I got a text from Moira relaying to me a conversation she'd just overheard between Sean and Tim as they were going to sleep in the next room.

"S: You like Gail? T: Yes, Sean. S: I love her; she's a good person. T: Yup. S: I miss her. You think she's a good person? T: Yes Sean, now go to sleep!" The sweetest guys ever!

What wonderful hospitality is always shown, no matter where I visit or what the occasion. The love and generosity that surrounded Sean throughout his life had the greatest impact on him. He learned to show love always! As much as all he learned about unconditional love from his mom and sisters, his love of sports definitely came from his dad. From Sean's participation in Special Olympics to his love and knowledge of the players on favorite teams, like the Yankees, Giants, and many college teams, too, he loved the games! I don't know many people who have been able to attend as many exciting sporting events as Sean, including Super Bowls and World Series games. It was a huge thrill for me to see Sean and his buddies march on to the field for the Special Olympics Games held in Trenton. His life was so rich, and he taught those of us who were privileged to be a part of his life SO MUCH!

Sean's life on earth may be over, but the impact he left and all the lessons that we learned from him will go on as long as we all remember to LIVE LIKE SEAN!

I believe Sean has been resurrected to eternal life and watches over us every day. I'll never forget him; I'll always miss him and love him until we meet again someday in God's great kingdom.

With much love and gratitude,
Gail Booth

To my children, their spouses, my grandchildren, and great-grandchildren,

In life we all will suffer disappointments, setbacks, and frustrations that are apt to anger us and cause a negative reaction on our part. I know, because I have been there many times. I will also confess that my negative reaction did not help diffuse the situation—no surprise there.

Now, though, I have learned a better way to react and cope with negative actions or situations. I learned this from a master teacher of joy and happiness, my grandson, Sean. Sean faced many obstacles in his life. I do not mean just the three Rs. I mean the negative actions and reactions of some people in social situations. I watched him wait and then smile broadly and sometimes just move on or other times enter into a short and pleasant conversation that left both people smiling happily.

Sean was always very aware of where he was and the attitude of those around him. If they appeared hostile or negative, he defused them and moved on. If they were sad, he empathized easily and made a friend. If they were friendly, he responded in kind with his big smile, sparkling eyes, and a kind word, a compliment.

We were all showered with Sean's kindness and love. His unconditional love. I know the meaning of "love"—love that I have for my wife, for my children, grandchildren, and great-grandchildren. I also know the meaning of "unconditional," as do you. But when I put the two words together, I realize now that combined they represent something more, something greater, and something more difficult to give.

I know it is not easy to give this kind of love, especially when faced with adversity, but Sean was a master at it, and hopefully so will we be if we follow his example. In my mind, Sean was a holy man, a true saint. Let us all learn from him.

Be kind. Be thoughtful. Be humble. Be empathetic. Be happy.

LIVE LIKE SEAN,

Papa Tim Nelligan

ABOUT THE AUTHOR

An entrepreneur, advocate, and published author, TJ Nelligan is a man of action who has made it his life's mission to serve and benefit others.

Nelligan founded his namesake company, Nelligan Sports Marketing, Inc. (NSM), in June 1999 with the mission of becoming the premier sports marketing company in the nation. As a result of his leadership, NSM's employees negotiated more than $500 million in sponsorship agreements with some of the country's best-known blue-chip companies. After 15 successful years, Nelligan sold his company to Learfield Sports in February 2014.

Before founding NSM, Nelligan spent nine years at Host Communications, Inc., including serving as president of Host's Sports Division and a member of Host's Senior Management Committee. Before joining Host, Nelligan gained sales and marketing experience with Procter & Gamble and spent seven years on Wall Street.

Having spearheaded some of the most successful marketing campaigns in collegiate sports, Nelligan looked to elevate the Special Olympics' status domestically and led the efforts to bring the

2014 Special Olympics USA Games to New Jersey. He then served as Chairman and CEO of the 2014 USA Games, where he oversaw all aspects of the event, including corporate partnerships, sports operations, event logistics, marketing, and public relations. Nelligan has been involved with Special Olympics New Jersey (SONJ) since 1995, serving on SONJ's Board of Directors from 1995 to 2011 and as Chairman of the Board from 2001 to 2003. As chairman, he raised millions of dollars for the Special Olympics New Jersey Sports Complex. Nelligan has also served on the board for both special-needs schools that his son, Sean, attended and helped raise money for both the Children's Center (now the P.G. Chambers School) and the Midland School.

An advocate for the needs of those with both intellectual and developmental disabilities, Nelligan served as Commissioner of the Commission of Higher Education for the State of New Jersey from 2005 to 2008. He was honored with the Man of the Year Award by SONJ in April 2007 at the SONJ annual gala. Montville Township High School inducted Nelligan into its Hall of Fame in 2004. Nelligan was named Montville Township Citizen of the Year in 2006 for his work with the special-needs population and the organizations that assist them.

Inspired by the sudden and tragic passing of his son, Sean, on Father's Day 2019, Nelligan wrote this book as a way to remember what an amazing person he was, and it gave him an opportunity to memorialize all of their experiences together. *Live Like Sean* allows the reader to witness the world through the eyes of a special-needs person and shows them that life lessons can come from the most unlikely places.

Nelligan is a graduate of the University of Richmond with a BA in economics.

NELLIGAN
2